The Healing
Between

William G. Heard

FOREWORD BY MAURICE FRIEDMAN

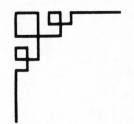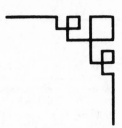

The Healing Between

A CLINICAL GUIDE

TO

DIALOGICAL PSYCHOTHERAPY

Jossey-Bass Publishers • San Francisco

Substantial discounts on bulk quantities of Jossey-Bass books are available to corporations, professional associations, and other organizations. For details and discount information, contact the special sales department at Jossey-Bass Inc., Publishers. (415) 433-1740; Fax (415) 433-0499.

For sales outside the United States, contact Maxwell Macmillan International Publishing Group, 866 Third Avenue, New York, New York 10022.

Manufactured in the United States of America

The paper used in this book is acid-free and meets the State of California requirements for recycled paper (50 percent recycled waste, including 10 percent postconsumer waste), which are the strictest guidelines for recycled paper currently in use in the United States.

The ink in this book is either soy- or vegetable-based and during the printing process emits fewer than half the volatile organic compounds (VOCs) emitted by petroleum-based ink.

Library of Congress Cataloging-in-Publication Data

Heard, William G., date.
    The healing between : a clinical guide to dialogical psychotherapy / William G. Heard. — 1st ed.
       p.   cm. — (The Jossey-Bass social and behavioral science series)
    Includes bibliographical references and index.
    ISBN 1-55542-589-5 (alk. paper)
    1. Pyschotherapist and patient. 2. Psychotherapy. I. Title. II. Series.
    [DNLM: 1. Psychotherapy—methods. 2. Professional–Patient Relations. 3. Verbal Behavior.   WM 420 H435h 1993]
RC480.8.H43   1993
616.89′14—dc20
DNLM/DLC
for Library of Congress   93-16060
                                                        CIP

FIRST EDITION
HB Printing   10 9 8 7 6 5 4 3 2 1   *Code 9388*

THE JOSSEY-BASS
SOCIAL AND BEHAVIORAL SCIENCE SERIES

To my wife Laura Grau

To my friend Elaine Threadgill
and
To my mentor Maurice Friedman

They stood with me in the writing of this book.

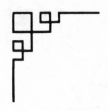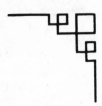

Contents

ix

**Part Two: Clinical Considerations
and Dialogical Psychotherapy**

15. Initial Client Contact and Treatment Goals   134

16. The Unfolding of the Treatment Process   142

     References and Suggested Readings   157

     Index   159

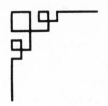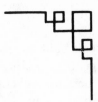

Foreword

In San Diego in the fall of 1991, William G. Heard entered the two-year training program of the Institute for Dialogical Psychotherapy, of which I am co-director. In the theory seminar that I conducted, Bill Heard stood out as the most determined of all the students. This was not only because of his thirty years of clinical experience and his doctoral training in empirical and behavioral psychology. It was also because of a peculiar tenacity of character that has made him one of the most challenging and gratifying postdoctoral students I have ever had. Heard not only went through the two years of our training program and attended our annual conferences, he also commuted several times a week to San Diego State University—where I was professor of religious studies, philosophy, and comparative literature—and saw me weekly for more than a year for private tutoring and discussion.

What concerned him most during those private meetings was working through each of the ten elements of dialogical psychotherapy that I had earlier articulated (Hycner, 1991; Friedman, 1992a). From this dialogue has emerged *The Healing Between*—an important book for dialogical psychotherapy and for psychotherapy in general. Dialogical psychotherapy focuses on the *meeting* between therapist and client as the central healing mode, whatever analysis, role-playing, or other therapeutic techniques or activities may be employed. Crucial to this form of therapy is the healing partnership that arises between the therapist and the client and between the client and other people.

This book serves as an easily accessible introduction for those who are unfamiliar with the movement of dialogical psychotherapy. It sets forth each element of the dialogical approach in a clear, concrete fashion, with illustrations from Heard's varied range of clinical experience. The book also represents a further development in our understanding and application of dialogical psychotherapy beyond the pioneering work of Hans Trüb, Leslie Farber, Ivan Bosormenyi-Nagy, Richard Hycner, Aleene Friedman, and myself (see References and Suggested Readings at the back of this book). In its dual role of introducing and advancing dialogical psychotherapy, *The Healing Between* broadens the audience for this therapeutic approach, which has had a profound impact on those of us who practice it and on our clients.

San Diego, California   Maurice Friedman
July 1993   *Professor Emeritus*
                                                   San Diego State University

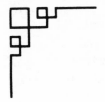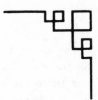

Preface

This book takes a different perspective than do most studies of human interaction. It concentrates on what happens *between* the people interacting rather than what happens *within* each person. Dialogical psychotherapy focuses on the interactions between client and therapist, the dialogue in which each partner embraces the wholeness of the other. The process has a profound effect on both partners of the interaction as their fragmented selves are brought together into an integrated whole. The restoration of wholeness makes growth possible and heals the sick psyche.

Background

The Healing Between is the result of my affiliation with the Institute for Dialogical Psychotherapy in San Diego. In 1988, I began attending the institute's annual meetings, at one of which I was introduced to the philosophical anthropology of Martin Buber, particularly his philosophy of dialogue. Buber contends that interactions generate a new reality—the *between*. Interested in learning more about these ideas, I sought out Maurice Friedman, co-director of the institute, and began a course of study with him that lasted for three years. Friedman had derived the elements of dialogical psychotherapy from Buber's philosophical anthropology (Friedman, 1985, 1992a), and although he had compared and contrasted the dialogical approach with other major approaches to psychotherapy in *The Healing Dialogue in Psychotherapy* (1985), no one had yet comprehensively discussed the elements of dialogical psychotherapy and given appropriate clinical examples of them. In the course of my studies with him, we agreed that I would write this book.

Scope and Treatment

Because no other books have attempted to explain and illustrate the elements of dialogical psychotherapy, *The Healing Between* is essentially an introductory work. I have attempted to apply the elements of dialogical psychotherapy in a pragmatic manner to address the therapeutic concerns of the clinician. I have tried to provide detailed and comprehensive treatment of the elements. Although the examples I have used are taken from actual practice, each is a composite of numerous experiences with different clients.

The reader may notice that the examples often portray short-term, problem-solving approaches. This does not imply that dialogical psychotherapy is not applicable to long-term, life-changing therapy; rather, it reflects the current practice of most mental health professionals, resulting from the demands of the managed health care system.

Purpose

The purpose of the book is to describe the elements of dialogical psychotherapy and illustrate their application in the clinical setting. My hope is to interest psychotherapists in using the dialogical approach in therapeutic endeavors—to introduce clinicians to the mysterious healing between that unfolds during dialogue. To work in the healing between, the clinician must be willing to encounter the raw existence of the client, to experience the real stuff of the client's life, without benefit of the theoretical screen that usually keeps us at a distance and allows us to assume an objective, professional stance. To experience a client's pain in such a direct, unmediated way can be threatening to the therapist, but I believe it is necessary to heal the client.

Audience

This book offers a fresh approach to psychotherapy and will be of interest to practicing mental health professionals and pastoral counselors. It is appropriate for graduate students in clinical psychology, social work, and family counseling. Faculty members teaching courses in the theory and practice of psychology and counseling will find it interesting and provocative. It is designed to serve as a supplemental textbook for such courses.

Overview of the Contents

In the Introduction, I tell the story of how experiences throughout my life have guided my journey to dialogical psychotherapy and to writing this book. Part One of the book presents the eleven elements of dialogical psychotherapy. Nine of these elements were elucidated by Friedman from Buber's work. Friedman himself developed the element of touchstones. In my study of Buber and the elements that Friedman presented, the eleventh, personal direction, emerged in my mind as an indispensable element. The first chapter presents the distinguishing characteristics of dialogical psychotherapy. The chapter stresses concern for the client's unique wholeness and discusses such matters as life purpose and meaning (as seen in the client's personal direction) and existential (as opposed to neurotic) guilt.

The following chapters look at each of the elements, with clinical examples illustrating their use in the therapeutic setting. Chapter Two explores the *between,* the new reality that is created when true dialogue occurs between the therapist and the client; it is in the between that healing takes place. Chapter Three explains the *dialogical* relationship: the special relationship that must exist between client and therapist for the between to come to life. *Distanc-*

ing and relating is presented in Chapter Four: a twofold movement that allows the therapist to set herself apart from the client and see him as a unique, whole person and relate to him as a whole rather than focusing on one trait or characteristic.

Chapter Five describes the *healing through meeting* that occurs in the between, when therapist and client are totally responsive to the new reality created between them. *Personal direction*, the focus of Chapter Six, is what comes from the healing between. It is unique to the client and points him towards achieving his potential. Chapter Seven examines *the unconscious*. Buber attributed three functions to the unconscious: (1) the entity synonymous with one's wholeness, (2) the guardian of that wholeness, and (3) the locus of psychic activities that have somehow broken apart from one's whole self (1967; see also Friedman, 1985). Chapter Eight deals with *dreams*. Although they are not one of the eleven elements of dialogical psychotherapy, dreams are an essential part of the unconscious and deserve separate consideration.

Inclusion, the topic of Chapter Nine, is the process by which the therapist must embrace the entire being of the client, thus experiencing his pain as though it were her own. Chapter Ten addresses *mutuality*, the openness and mutual trust that client and therapist must have toward one another to achieve a dialogue. The therapist's challenge is to acknowledge that the client is not required to reciprocate the total inclusion of the other for which she must strive. *Confirmation*, the subject of Chapter Eleven, involves the therapist's helping the client to find personal direction, the fulfillment of his uniqueness.

Chapter Twelve explores *existential guilt*, the guilt that comes from knowing we have consciously hurt another and have thus alienated ourselves from the common order of society. Finally, Chapter Thirteen articulates the importance of *touchstones*, which are what each partner in the dialogue takes away from the experience.

Part Two of the book deals with clinical considerations associated with the dialogical approach. The first chapter in the part, Chapter Fourteen, examines the attitudes necessary to effect dialogue in therapy. Obstacles to therapeutic dialogue, which exist in both the therapist and the client, are described in detail. Chapter

Fifteen presents dialogical considerations associated with the initial client contact and treatment goals. This chapter outlines the dialogical psychotherapist's concerns for the client, which exceed those of practitioners of more traditional approaches. In Chapter Sixteen, the final chapter, the distinctiveness of the dialogical process is discussed. The chapter looks at the mysterious nature of the unfolding of the between in the therapeutic process. In closing, reference is made to the areas in which the dialogical approach needs to be extended. These include exploration of dialogue as it unfolds in the between; the dialogue in early childhood, with its implications for developmental psychology; inclusion and confirmation as they relate to transference and countertransference in the therapeutic setting; further exploration of the unconscious from the dialogical perspective; and the etiology of psychopathology and its relationship to dialogue.

Acknowledgments

I am most grateful to the numerous clients who have shared their lives with me. Because of our dialogues, the unique stamp of each of them has enriched my own wholeness. Without Maurice Friedman's confidence in me, this book would not have been written. The other co-directors of the Dialogical Institute, James De Leo and Richard Hycner, were also extremely helpful in reading and offering suggestions for changes in the manuscript. I also would not have finished the book without the help and encouragement of my wife, Laura Grau. She was always ready to listen and encourage me in spite of the demands of her own clinical practice and ongoing training. I am deeply indebted to Elaine Threadgill, who is my friend, professional colleague, and office manager. She listened patiently each day as I read her what I had written the day before. I thank each of these people for giving me their understanding and concern. I would also like to acknowledge Rebecca McGovern and Lasell Whipple, senior acquisitions editor and project editor at Jossey-Bass, respectively, and copyeditor Patterson Lamb for their efforts. It has been a joy to work with them.

Finally, I acknowledge that the book is based mostly on the ideas of those who have preceded me. May the words of Pascal serve as my defense: "Let no one say I said nothing new; my arrangement of matter is new. . . . I had just as soon be told that I use old terms. And as if the same words differently arranged did not form a different discourse, just as the same words differently arranged form different thoughts!" (Pascal, [1676] 1965, p. 369).

San Juan Capistrano, California   William G. Heard
July 1993

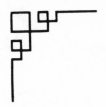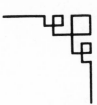

The Author

William G. Heard is a licensed clinical psychologist in the state of California. He received his B.A. degree (1957) from Grand Canyon College in history and his M.A. and Ph.D. degrees (1960 and 1964) from Arizona State University in psychology.

   Heard's activities in psychology over a period of twenty-eight years have included teaching, program administration and development, community organization at both the state and county levels, and clinical practice. He has worked as a clinical and program administrator in the areas of drug abuse, alcoholism, and mental health, with consultation, outpatient, day-care, and inpatient services. He has served as clinical director of a free-standing psychiatric hospital and for the last eleven years has been involved in full-time private practice in San Juan Capistrano, California.

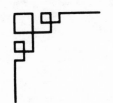 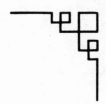

The Healing
Between

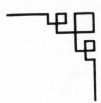

Introduction

My journey to dialogical psychotherapy and the writing of this book has been circuitous and long, but always I was guided by an interest in the practical: what works. Another trait shared by my personal philosophy and the philosophical basis of the dialogical approach is a profound regard for each person's uniqueness. I first became aware of this uniqueness when I was going to school and supporting my family as a lay pastor in Baptist churches. I was constantly amazed by people's ability to cope with the problems of living, always in their own individual and special ways. Later, I became a believing humanist, some thirty years before I read Buber's wonderful essay, "Believing Humanism" (Buber, 1967, pp. 117–122), and learned of his philosophical anthropology and his concept of the "I-Thou" dialogue, which is the foundation of dialogical psychotherapy.

All of these beliefs that are so fundamental to my thinking were severely tested during my training as a psychologist. I wanted to be a clinical psychologist, but I was told that to be a good clinician I must know all areas of psychology. These were the times

1

of B. F. Skinner and behavioral psychology. I was taught that psychology was the science of behavior, and behavior alone. It did not matter whether the behavior was that of a flatworm or a person. I was immersed in statistics, research design, scientific methodology, and learning principles. Each time I suggested taking clinical classes I was counseled to wait and advised that we did not know enough about behavioral principles to apply them to complex human behavior.

As a graduate student, I learned that anything that could not be studied via the scientific method was not worthy of study. I heard students told that if they continued to use such mentalistic terms as "mind" they would be asked to leave the class. There was a brain, but no one could scientifically study a mind. One could only study the behavior of an organism that had an organ called a brain.

I was told that the only way I could receive a doctoral degree was to continue my specialization in general and experimental psychology. If I wished to pursue my interest in clinical psychology, I must do it later. Clinical psychology was considered voodoo at best, and a doctoral student should not be allowed to waste his training in the practice of applied psychology. It was under these conditions that I received my doctoral degree in the summer of 1964 and went into the real world.

After two years of teaching and doing research, I was able to move toward clinical psychology. I was offered a two-year clinical internship, arranged by the state's Mental Health Department, with the agreement that I would return to the department as a consulting psychologist. After completing the internship, I began seeing clients in a part-time private practice while also working for the state. During the years I worked for public agencies I was able to establish what have become model facilities for the care of the indigent mentally ill. I helped develop a social detoxification unit for alcoholics and expanded my knowledge of program development and administration. All of this was very different from the detached scientific observance I had learned in graduate school.

After entering private clinical practice full-time, I enrolled in the training program of the Institute for Dialogical Psychotherapy in San Diego. In the first year, I was captured by Martin Buber's philosophical anthropology. It spoke to a spiritual need I had neglected since my frustration with academic psychology and rejection of institutionalized religion.

In studying Buber's philosophy, I realized I had become the victim of the I–It relationships of the scientific world. I had longed for a world that was logical and pragmatic; my clinical theories and approaches were explicit—but inadequate. I performed the clinical function but had no heart for it. I was plagued by deep doubts and struggled to overcome my skepticism. I was aware of a serious misfit. It always seemed to me that when I really helped a client it was because of something personal I brought to the encounter and not something from my psychological training. I felt guilty because in these meetings there was a realness that did not seem to belong in the clinical setting. I now realize that it was only on such occasions that true healing was taking place as I made direct contact with the client's actual existence and not some theoretical notion.

In my study of Buber, I have come to realize that the prediction and control of human behavior that science seeks by objectivization cannot encompass humanness. Our essence as human beings can be met only in the encounter of the raw stuff of personal existence in the house of dialogue that has become my new home.

In exploring the client-therapist dialogue, I have tried to remain mindful of our need for predictable clinical techniques. Yet the real work of healing does not occur in the skillful application of techniques but in the mystery of what is generated in the interactions between us and our clients.

I invite you to join me in the pursuit of dialogue in psychotherapy. The richness of dialogue can be experienced only in its occurrence. The dialogical approach protects us from self-aggrandizement. It demands a humility that takes us beyond our self-serving inclinations and requires us to commit our whole selves to the concerns of our clients. The healing of the dialogue comes by grace. When it is corrupted, what was between us and another quietly slips away and we enter once again into the I–It world of relating. When through acceptance and inclusion we can create a meeting between ourselves and a client, the power to heal that emerges can be truly extraordinary. I hope this book will be a door that opens dialogical psychotherapy to you.

PART ONE

The Elements
of
Dialogical
Psychotherapy

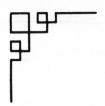
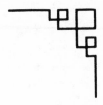

1

The Importance of
Dialogical Psychotherapy

Dialogical psychotherapy is based on the philosophical anthropology of Martin Buber (1878–1965), a renowned Jewish religious scholar, philosopher, and writer. It is different from other approaches in that it embraces in its perspective all aspects of our existence—including our ontology, the examination of our being. It considers our humanness not as an assortment of aspects but as a whole. This view contrasts with studies that focus on pieces of our existence—physical, psychological, social, cultural, historical, and spiritual. Each of these ways of viewing the human creature has spawned a separate discipline with its own methodology designed to study systematically those aspects peculiar to its particular point of view. This compartmentalizing, however, is not congruent with the way we experience our existence.

None of these sciences has concerned itself with man in his wholeness—the core of philosophical anthropology (Farber, cited in Friedman, 1992b, p. 211). It is in this discipline that the totality of a person's existence is central. Martin Buber has presented a philosophical anthropology that encompasses the wholeness of our

7

lives in a manner that matches how we experience life. He contends
that to understand our wholeness we must understand the nature of
our being and the primordial givens from which our humanness
evolves, that is, our ontology—the experience of our existence that
is determined by the nature of our being as human beings (Buber,
1988, pp. 3–10; Friedman, 1992, pp. 127–131). Buber has carefully
thought out and articulated these ontological givens in his philosophical anthropology. All the characteristics of our humanness
flow from and are shaped by them. These ontological givens are
presented in the elements of dialogical psychotherapy: specifically,
the between, distancing and relating, and our need for confirmation. All the other elements derive from these givens.

Personal Wholeness

The dialogical psychotherapist must be concerned with the client's
whole existence. She believes that when all aspects of the client's
existence are integrated, he experiences himself as a coherent whole.
This integration creates mental health. When various aspects of his
existence are not integrated, his wholeness is fragmented, and he is
dysfunctional.

The client can never be completely whole; his wholeness is
not a once-and-for all state of being. It is not a static condition; it
comes and goes in a dynamic fashion. The client may bring his total
potential to his response to a specific event in his life; then, in that
instance, in that particular moment, he is whole. But he cannot
maintain that state. The dialogical psychotherapist's task is to help
the client approach wholeness.

The client's personal wholeness is realized only in his relationships with others. The dialogical psychotherapist holds that the
client's personal wholeness can be realized in his relationship with
the therapist. The manner in which they relate determines the extent to which the client experiences unity. To achieve this complete-
ness requires a special way of interacting that generates a new
reality in the exchange between the client and the therapist, one that
does not exist in either apart from their relating. The healing in the
client does not come from the therapist nor from within the client
himself but from this new reality generated in their interaction. Its

appearance is under the control of neither and its power to heal is a mystery. The healing between is an ontological given that makes it possible for the therapist to interact with the client in a manner that integrates and unifies the client's fragmented self.

The Nature of Dialogical Psychotherapy

Dialogical psychotherapy attempts to articulate the struggles in our human existence that have their origin in who we are. This attempt has resulted in an approach to psychotherapy that is compatible with the ontological issues of the client's life. Issues such as purpose, meaning, and personal direction in the client's life are translated into elements that can be used in the therapeutic endeavor. The approach allows us to see each person as a unique individual as this picture unfolds in the dialogue. It is an image of the human that is not found in our individual psychology but in our relationship with others. It comes from a new reality, the between, that is beyond the imagination and the expectations of both the client and the therapist. It reveals not only what the client is now but also what he can uniquely become, and it empowers him to pursue it.

Dialogical psychotherapy demands a commitment and involvement with the client that may place the therapist in harm's way. She must be willing to experience the client's existence as though it were her own in spite of the psychic pain it may cause her. She is asked to expose herself to the mysterious healing work of the between. She must enter her relationship with the client totally dependent and accepting of the direction that arises from it without foreknowledge or control of what may come forth.

The dialogical psychotherapist seeks to relate to the client in a way that is beyond her conventional perceptions, in a way that cannot be categorized. She seeks a relationship with the client's uniqueness, which cannot be captured and analyzed by her cognitive abilities. The client's uniqueness does not and cannot exist in her understanding. It exists in the reality between her and the client and cannot be comprehended. It is a mystery that can be apprehended only as it unfolds in the healing between the two of them.

Dialogical psychotherapy focuses on the uniqueness as well as the wholeness of the client. The approach contends that the purpose of the client's life is to fulfill his uniqueness, which unfolds in the dialogue. Thus, the meaning of our existence is not found in our psychological selves but in our dialogical selves.

Elements of Dialogical Psychotherapy

The ontological givens of Buber's philosophical anthropology are reflected in the elements of dialogical psychotherapy that were first presented by Maurice Friedman (Hycner, 1991, pp. ix–xi; Friedman, 1992b, pp. 55-57). The elements are the between, the dialogical, distancing and relating, healing through meeting, personal direction, the unconscious, inclusion, the problematic of mutuality, confirmation, existential guilt, and touchstones. Nine of the elements presented by Friedman came directly from Buber's philosophical anthropology. I added "personal direction," which is also drawn from Buber's work. Friedman developed "touchstones." Although not a concept of Buber, it is compatible with his philosophical anthropology.

The elements are discussed in detail with clinical examples in subsequent chapters. A synopsis of them is given here to emphasize the uniqueness of dialogical psychotherapy in contrast to other approaches to the therapeutic endeavor. The elements embody the means by which the therapist implements the concerns of the dialogical approach.

The first element is the *between*. The dialogical psychotherapist contends that it is in the reality of the between that the important therapeutic work is accomplished. The between is the basic element of the approach, and the efficacy of the other elements stems from it. It is a reality generated in the interaction between the partners of a special type of relationship. The special way of relating that generates the healing between is called the *dialogical* relationship. The *dialogical* element is our door to the between. It is the method used by the dialogical psychotherapist to engage the client in the therapeutic endeavor. Because of its central importance it is the workhorse of the approach.

The pair of ontological givens that make the dialogical possible, *distancing and relating,* are the third element. Understanding how these givens shape us is crucial to the dialogue. The manner in which we relate after distancing determines whether we will interact with the other as an object (It) or as a subject (Thou).

The context in which the healing between does its work is the meeting, the *healing through meeting.* The meeting is made possible by the dialogue and is the conduit for the healing between. This element focuses on the meeting of the therapist and the client as the means of healing. Healing does not result from something the therapist does to the client: it comes from their meeting.

The dialogical psychotherapist contends that when the client experiences his wholeness in his interactions with the world he finds direction in his life that brings purpose and meaning to his existence. In such interactions the client also undergoes an empowerment that facilitates the pursuit of his personal direction. This element, *personal direction,* does not imply a universal image of mankind that each client is supposed to live up to. On the contrary, each client is unique, and it is in the fulfillment of his uniqueness that he finds his personal direction.

To recapitulate, the client's personal direction emerges from those interactions to which he brings his wholeness. The manner in which this takes place is of special interest to dialogical psychotherapists. It is their contention that with the client, as with all human beings, personal direction is an aspect of one's existence that is pre-dialogical. That is, it is not available to the client prior to dialogue. It is an unconscious potential until it is called out by the meeting. Although most of us have been afforded sufficient experiences of dialogue that enable us to find our personal direction, this is often not so in the case of the client. Dialogical psychotherapy seeks to afford the client opportunity for such dialogue. The implications of this pre-dialogical potential are discussed in the element labeled *the unconscious.*

One of the conditions for the dialogue's occurrence is the therapist's ability to make the client present and accessible to her awareness in a manner that makes the client's existence, in that moment, as real as her own. Buber tells us, "Such an awareness is impossible, however, if and so long as the other [client] is the separated object of my contemplation or even observation, for this wholeness and its centre do not let themselves be known to contemplation or observation. It is only possible when I step into an elemental relation with the other [client], that is, when he becomes present to me" (Buber, 1988, p. 70). In order to accomplish this task, we must develop and exercise a gift that resides as a potential in our innermost being. Buber calls this gift "imagining the real": "In its essential being this gift is not a looking at the other, but a bold swinging—demanding the most intense stirring of one's being—into the life of the other" (Buber, 1988, p. 71). Imagining the real is to experience the client's presence before you as a real person in all his unique, unified wholeness without analysis or abstraction. When this occurs the therapist experiences in the most personal way the subjective world of the client; at the same time she remains apart from the client by being fully aware of her own existence as completely separate and different. This element is labeled *inclusion*.

In the treatment setting, the therapist and the client have an unusual relationship that is not reciprocal in all respects. There may be mutual contact, trust, and concern for the issues addressed in the dialogue, but there is not mutual inclusion. Because of the nature of the therapeutic relationship it is not appropriate for the therapist to expect the client to regard her problems in the same manner as she does his. The therapist does not come for help; it is the client who seeks help. This issue is addressed under the element *problem of mutuality*.

Confirmation, the next element, emerges from the dialogue and is used by the therapist to support the client in the pursuit of his personal direction, that is, to fulfill his uniqueness in the situation the dialogue addresses. It is the method used by the therapist to support the healing changes in the client that occur in the dialogue. Often the therapist must point out to the client those aspects of his life that are not in tune with the dialogue. Confirmation is a very powerful tool of the psychotherapist and must always be directed by the dialogue.

When the client does not appropriately address the issues raised in the dialogue, there is the danger of incurring *existential guilt*. This is guilt that arises when the client has consciously hurt someone and thereby has injured the order of the world. If by his own conduct he has thwarted the expression of another's uniqueness, he is existentially guilty. When he is the victim of an injury by another, as opposed to being the perpetrator of the injury, he may experience guilt feelings, but it is a neurotic guilt. Dialogical psychotherapy distinguishes between two kinds of guilt, existential, in which the client is truly guilty, and neurotic, in which the client feels guilty but is blameless.

The last element, *touchstones,* deals with the reality coming from the dialogue that the client retains. There are two ways of viewing touchstones: those that emerge from the dialogue and those that we take to the dialogue.

Throughout the client's dialogical history touchstones emerge from his dialogues to be carried with him to future dialogues. These touchstones embody the unique reality of the client, and as this reality changes, the touchstones are constantly in the process of being altered in each successive dialogue.

Summation and Preview

From this short description, the reader is not expected to have an adequate understanding and appreciation of the elements as they are applied in the therapeutic encounter. However, I hope that he or she has caught a glimpse of the issues on which the elements focus and perhaps a hint of the distinctiveness of dialogical psychotherapy. In the following chapter I will discuss the first element of dialogical psychotherapy, the *between,* which is the foundation on which the other elements rest.

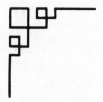
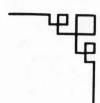

2

The
Between

The dynamics of dialogical psychotherapy come from the reality, the *between*, that is generated between the partners of a special kind of relationship. The therapeutic efficacy of the other elements is dependent on it, and the restoration of the client's wholeness is contingent on its presence in the therapeutic encounter. Without its presence, healing cannot take place.

The Distinctive Element

The between is the distinctive element of the dialogical approach, and its healing presence is a mystery to us. If we consider the nature of the world, there are many comparable mysteries. For example, the mysterious appearance of a new substance produced by the interaction of two molecules of hydrogen and one molecule of oxygen is analogous to the mystery of the between. The interaction of these two chemical elements generates a new reality—water. Yet prior to their interaction there is nothing in either that would lead us to anticipate such a result. Taken individually, these elements perform

14

entirely separate functions in the world, Hydrogen is so inflammable that we have ceased using it in our lighter-than-aircraft balloons and dirigibles. The presence of oxygen is essential for combustion to take place. Yet when hydrogen and oxygen are combined in the appropriate manner they generate water, which is often used to stifle combustion. Our familiarity with this phenomenon does not diminish its mystery.

An even more profound mystery is life itself, which emerges from the unique combination of matter under appropriate conditions. Scientists can ponder the various types of matter and the characteristics of the conditions under which this new reality appears, but their deductions cannot tell us why life appears. Our pursuit of the answer simply takes us to the next level of how. Such reductionism only postpones the mystery.

The Importance of Why

The deterministic approach of the natural sciences finds the answer to why something happens to us in an objective explanation of how it happens, but this is not a satisfactory answer to those of us seeking to understand our personal existence. I may be told how I became infected with tuberculosis, but what I really want to know most of all is why me? Why was I in that place, in that condition, at that time? Subjectively, it is not *how* things happen to us that perplexes us, but *why* they happen. We cannot find the purpose and meaning of our personal existence in how things happen to us. We want to know why.

The dialogical approach contends that finding the why of personal existence is crucial to the well-being of the client. The client is not satisfied with an answer that says "that's just how the world is." The healing answer is found in a reality that lies beyond the subjective reality of the client—the reality of the between. The mystery is that the source of the client's healing is not found within himself nor the therapist, but between them.

The Third Reality

The ontological given that two persons—two individual existences with two separate subjective realities—can meet with each other and in their interaction generate a new reality between them is the foundation of Buber's philosophical anthropology. He contended that in addition to the reality experienced by either side of a relationship, there is a third reality that arises in their interaction with each other (Buber, 1988, p. 65). This reality—the between—is distinct from the reality of either of the partners of the relationship (Buber, 1958, p. 33). The given reality of both partners of the relationship has been altered by existential grace: "A grace that cannot be planned nor counted on, however much it is helped along" (Friedman, 1992a, p. 108). It is "the grace that comes to us from the other who meets us but also from our own resources, which are not simply waiting for us to use them but come and go, only partially subject to our will" (Friedman, 1992a, p. 203) "and moves between the client and therapist" (p. 220). Neither of the partners can generate nor manipulate this reality. Each can only attempt to create the conditions for its appearance and hope it occurs. To grasp this reality results in profound changes for those involved in the relationship. Buber contended that to the extent we experience the reality of the between, we become truly human (Buber, 1988, p. 74). It is in the between, in our special relationship with another, that we find our humanness.

The appearance of the between is contingent on the therapist relating to the client in a special manner. That is, the therapist embraces the wholeness of the client by imagining what is real for him. Although Buber extends the possibility of relating in this manner to others, we will restrict our considerations to those relationships that take place between the client and the therapist. Buber calls this special way of establishing a world of relations "I-Thou" (Buber, 1958, p. 6). It requires that each partner focus his wholeness on the other in such a way that the other is experienced in all of his uniqueness. Neither sees the other as a type or a category to be analyzed. The other is experienced as Thou.

The Need for Wholeness

An example of the wholeness we must bring to this special relationship is seen in a young child's behavior, which displays a total lack of self-consciousness. In most instances, as adults, we do not experience our wholeness. We are fragmented in our response to the world. However, there are instances in our adult life when wholeness occurs. When you are walking, unaware of the natural smoothness of your stride as your arms move freely back and forth by your side, in that moment you are whole. However, something happens the moment you notice how each arm moves back and forth in a natural rhythm paralleling the movement of the opposite leg. The rhythm is broken and in that moment you are fragmented and not whole in your walking. We cannot experience our wholeness and reflect on it at the same time. If while dancing, you are totally absorbed in the flow of the music to the exclusion of self-consciousness, at that moment you are whole. However, the moment you become conscious of what is happening, there is an awkwardness that you did not feel in the moments before. You have lost your wholeness and become fragmented by setting aside a part of your self to notice what is happening. We experience our wholeness as an unmediated sense of being in those moments when we respond to a concrete event.

The awareness of our personal wholeness is a knowing that cannot be rationally analyzed. By its very nature it cannot be related to as an object and defined. It is a Thou that in its uniqueness defies description. It encompasses all that a person is and all that a person can be, which cannot be apprehended until it unfolds in the concrete event.

The fragmentation of the client's wholeness, in contrast, can be defined, for it is seen in the symptoms that reflect the disturbance that has brought him to therapy. We may experience the consequence of the client's wholeness in his reactions to the dialogue, for example, his movement from resentment to forgiveness, fear to serenity, rejection to acceptance, and so on. The disturbed client displays behavior of which he was not previously capable, indicating healing is taking place. This will be seen in the clinical examples that are presented throughout the book.

Our I–Thou relationships are not like our relationships in which the other is treated as an object. In most of our relationships, I–It, the other is regarded as a thing to be understood, to be analyzed and categorized for later appropriate use. The other's uniqueness is of no value. We relate to the other only as we can fit him into a general category. The other's possibilities for being are of concern to us only as they have relevance for meeting our needs. When we encounter a person at the checkout stand, a waitress, or a mechanic, we often view him or her only in terms of the particular function we want performed. At that moment, we relate to that person not as a person but as an object. In such I-It relationships there is no *between* in the dialogical sense, although there is always a potential for the between to appear if the relationship should evolve into an I-Thou interaction.

Case Examples

From the dialogical perspective, the healing work of psychotherapy is found in the between of our I-Thou interactions and not in ourselves as therapists. Healing is not something we as therapists do to the client nor is it something the client accomplishes within himself. The source of the client's healing is in the reality between the therapist and himself, which is created by their interaction. This reality, the between, is the dynamic of the therapeutic relationship and the therapist who avoids working in it cannot be effective. This can be seen in my treatment of a client whom I will call Jay.

I was asked by Jay to assist him in his attempts to reconcile with his wife. Jay had been married for about twelve years and had four children. Both of his parents had been alcoholics. He had one older sister who had recently committed suicide. Jay was emotionally dependent on his wife and was finding it very difficult to tolerate her absence from his life. Her leaving had severely depressed him. Just prior to his coming to see me, she had informed him of her intent to divorce him.

Jay was extremely upset and wept throughout the initial portion of the interview. He stated that he did not want to continue living without his wife. I could say or do nothing to console him. I felt helpless and inept. I thought, as his therapist, I should be able to make him feel better, but all I could do was feel his deep anguish. He spoke of feeling the same way he had when he was a small boy lying in bed at night weeping while he listened to his parents fight. He described feeling all alone with no one to care for him. As he sat slumped over on the couch before me, I ached for him.

My first impulse was to escape his pain by analyzing what he had done to get himself into such an emotional state. I consoled myself with the thought that it was his fault. After all, he had done the things that had prompted his wife to leave him. I remembered a previous session in which his wife had told me that he had become extremely controlling and distancing as a ploy to hold on to her. When she could no longer stand the isolation, she left him. He had entered the marriage with such strong dependency needs, as a result of the absence of nurturing in his early childhood, that the marriage never had a chance.

I began feeling better. I had been able by my silent analysis to separate myself from the pain I had been sharing with Jay. I thought, now that I understand Jay's problem, I can begin to function as a therapist. I will help Jay to understand the cause of his dilemma. In truth, what I had done was to remove myself from the between that had been present from moment to moment as I had shared Jay's pain. I had withdrawn to seek my own comfort, leaving Jay to struggle alone; in the process I had subjected him to what he feared most: abandonment. Jay's healing work could not be done by me, the therapist, nor by himself as he listened and accepted my interpretation. The healing had to be accomplished in the interaction between us. This became evident as I tried to explain to Jay the cause of his dilemma. Jay indicated that he understood and accepted what I was saying, but it did not help.

At this point in the session, I realized that the most helpful thing I could do for Jay was to share his feelings and thoughts rather than interpret them—to return to the type of interaction with Jay that produced something between us that would generate healing. From time to time during the latter part of the session, as I remained with Jay in his hurtful place, I could sense his relief as subtle changes occurred in his countenance and body language. By the close of the session I noticed a discernible difference in his demeanor. He was much more animated and spoke more freely. Before leaving, he said he felt much better although he could not understand why since the same conditions still prevailed in his life. The dynamic of Jay's healing was not found in either of us but in the reality between us that had been created by our interaction.

The between thrusts the reality of the client on the therapist in a manner that is sometimes almost overwhelming. I experienced such an encounter with the between while seeing a mother and father with their thirteen-year-old son, Al. Both parents were perplexed with their son's behavior. They had not encountered such actions with their seven other children and they were uncertain about what they should do.

As I listened to their description of their son's behavior, I was struck by their bewilderment. They could not put their finger on the problem although they knew there was something wrong. They thought he might still be using speed, although he did not present any signs of drug abuse. According to the mother, he had done odd jobs for an older man who may have introduced him to pornography. However, no girlie magazines had been found in his room. The father worried about his son's selling body surfing boards (boogie boards) to other youngsters in the community. He was worried that his son was selling them for much more than they were worth. Yet, his son had been successful and had encountered no difficulties. The only substantive indications that something might be wrong was his having been caught with amphetamines at school and being placed in special classes. He was currently having difficulty keeping up with his studies but was getting C's in his classes. He had never been a good student. I found myself being caught up in the parents' bewilderment. The only plausible reason they could give for their concern was their son's past behavior and their fear of what he might do in the future.

In my interaction with Al, there was no manifestation of hostility. He was polite but not very verbal. He did not seem to be depressed or anxious. I could not get a handle on the situation. I thought, "How can I help this adolescent?" What is wrong with him?" Then it struck me: he was as bewildered as his parents. They must have been picking up his confusion. As we continued our interaction, it became increasingly apparent that he knew as little about what was wrong with him as his parents.

At this point I asked Al to support me in working with his parents. I explained to him that because of their concern for him they would continue to bug him about what was wrong until they felt better about him. He agreed and we began to meet with his parents. In the sessions, I always identified with him and sought to assist him in talking to his parents in a way that assured them that he was all right. As the sessions continued, I became more and more attuned to the manner in which he experienced himself in the world. Finally, in one of the later sessions, I suddenly experienced the source of Al's bewilderment. This young man was caught in the grip of fear. He was frightened of life and all that he could not understand. This fear was prompted by something more than just growing up; it was associated with his very existence. In that moment I felt his fear and was struck by its awesome power as it swept over me. I was so overcome by the feeling that I immediately turned to him and said, "Al, you are frightened." A look of relief spread over his face; at last, someone understood his problem—although I think he was as surprised as I by discovering what was wrong.

In subsequent sessions the parents spoke of Al's fondness for me. I was the only therapist he had seen that he believed understood and listened to him. Yet the source of the discovery that impressed him was not found in me or him but in the interactions between us.

In the cases of both Jay and Al, we can distinguish how the between works in the therapeutic setting. Both clients were affected in a healing manner. It is important to recognize that this does not mean that healing can only take place between the therapist and the client. Whenever people meet and imagine what is real for each other in their relating there is the possibility of healing. It is just that most clients are so injured and fragmented that others find it too threatening or difficult to imagine what is real for them. However, the healing of the between is not under the control of the therapist. He can only hope it appears in his interactions with the client. When it fails to emerge, the experience can be very frustrating, particularly after the therapist has experienced its presence in other therapeutic endeavors. It produces such a powerful impact that the therapist's own efforts tend to pale in comparison. It also requires that we redefine the issues associated with what has been called *transference* and *countertransference*. However, these redefinitions lie beyond the scope of this book.

Summation and Preview

The reality of the between is not only the dynamic of dialogical psychotherapy but also its catalyst. Without it, the other elements of the dialogical approach are ineffective and there is no substantive power to bind them into a comprehensive whole. An appreciation of the dynamic is essential to mastering the other elements of dialogical psychotherapy, for each of these is designed to facilitate the work of the between.

In the next chapter, I discuss the dialogical—the method by which we enter the between. Frequently I will refer to the dialogical as justification for the therapist's activities with the client. Unless there is a clear understanding of the dialogical, the reader may feel that the therapist takes liberties that are inappropriate in treating the client.

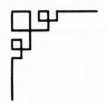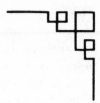

3

The
Dialogical

Buber calls the unfolding of the sphere of the between, "the dialog-ical" (Buber, 1988, p. 16). The dialogical is the expression of a special kind of relationship in which our interaction embraces the wholeness of the other by imagining what is real for him. When this occurs there is a new healing reality, the between, generated in the interaction.

The dialogical psychotherapist believes that it is in dialogue that our humanness evolves, whether it is between mother and child, wife and husband, family members, teacher and student, friends, employers, strangers, or members of the community. The dialogue is found in the multitude of ways we humans make contact with one another. It may be subtle or it may be explicit. It may be a look, a glance, a touch, an embrace, or a conversation. It is crucial to our development as human beings. Serious impairments are found in the lives of individuals who have not experienced suffi-cient dialogue. When this occurs these individuals become emotion-ally and mentally disturbed and often cannot function in society, at least to their fullest potential. Such persons are so disturbed that the average individual finds them too difficult to interact with. The absence of dialogue in their past tends to make future dialogue with them uncomfortable and unlikely. The dialogical psychotherapist holds that if these persons are to be healed, dialogue must be made available to them; for it is in dialogue that healing of their disturbance takes place.

The dialogical psychotherapist does not hold that she is the only source of healing dialogue for an emotionally and mentally ill person. There have always been sympathetic and understanding individuals who have functioned in this capacity with disturbed friends. There have always been others, such as the shaman, the medicine man, the priest, and the pastor, now and in times past, who have specialized in dialogue. The dialogue is common to all mankind and has been throughout history, whether it has been the mystic communing with his God as an absolute other or a mother cooing to her baby. Dialogue is not limited to so-called therapeutic encounters, nor is it limited to dialogical psychotherapy. Whenever and wherever humans relate to one another with the wholeness of their being in an I-Thou relationship, healing may result from their dialogue. All of us at one time or another have needed the healing that comes from dialogue.

Certainly other therapeutic approaches have utilized the dialogue in psychotherapy. Friedman has devoted the first half of his book *The Healing Dialogue in Psychotherapy* (Friedman, 1985) to exploring how other approaches have viewed the dialogue in psychotherapy. However, the contention that healing comes from the reality of the between generated by genuine dialogue is a distinction of the dialogical approach to psychotherapy. This recognition has led the dialogical psychotherapist to focus on the nature of dialogue and to seek out those elements that promote its occurrence in the therapeutic encounter. The self is never sick alone but always in a situation between it and other existing beings (Buber, 1967, p. 142). Friedman tells us that dialogue is characterized by mutuality, directness, presentness, intensity, and ineffability (Buber, 1988, p. 2).

Characteristics of the Dialogical

The relationship is mutual in that both partners share a common experience. However, the experience that is shared is greater than the sum of what either side brings to the relationship and different from either partner's separate experience. In fact, the experience does not have its origin in the individual realm of either partner but rather in a realm created by their interaction.

The experience of the between comes directly to each of the partners of the relationship without contemplation—prior to any cognitive processing. It is a knowing that is immediate without anticipation or interpretation. Its meaning goes straight to the core of both partners and alters their individual reality. Its appearance makes known what has been concealed in their individual existences. It is a knowing that neither can acquire by their individual efforts. It is a gift bestowed on them by the relationship.

Presentness is one of the distinguishing traits of this special relationship. Its presence excludes the experience of time. The past and the future are excluded from the experience. In those moments when the between is at work, the partners experience only the present. The experience is full and complete in itself without either of the partners needing to look backward to its beginning nor forward to its outcome. Its meaning is known in the immediate experience without reference to its time and place "for the meeting is not in space and time but time and space in meeting" (Friedman, 1960, p. 58).

The intensity of the experience can be seen in its profound influence on each of the partners in the relationship. The depth of the experience absorbs their whole existence. Its intensity precludes any other experience but itself and takes precedence over all the other aspects of their existence.

In addition to the characteristics of mutuality, directness, presentness and intensity, the experience of this special way of relating is ineffable. We may discuss how the experience impacts the partners of the relationship, but we cannot describe the event itself. We are presented with a dilemma that is paradoxical. We are talking about something that cannot be talked about without changing what it is. True dialogue is an I–Thou relationship; that is, it is the interaction of each of the partners as a Thou. We may describe the conditions that must have prevailed for the occurrence of such a relationship and describe what happens as a result of its occurrence, but when we attempt to describe the interaction itself we must respond in an I-It manner, making a Thou into an It for the purpose of description. While we can know this event in the meeting itself in communicating it to others, we cannot define it but only point to it. Each moment of the dialogue is a unique event that defies description. It is a reality that does not exist within either of the partners, nor is it a reality that is common to both partners: it is shared between them. The healing experience of the dialogue arises from a third reality that emerges in the interaction between the partners—the between.

The I-Thou relation which is necessary for genuine dialogue requires the therapist to become involved with the wholeness of the client. When the therapist directs her attention to the symptoms of the client, she is no longer relating to the client as a whole. She has restricted her interaction to a limited characteristic of the client and cannot expect the healing work of the between to be present in her therapeutic endeavors. The therapist must remain open to the totality of the client.

The Need for Reciprocity

However, the initiation of the dialogue does not reside entirely in the efforts of the therapist. It requires a reciprocal interaction involving both the client and the therapist. Yet, a part of the client's injury that brought him to therapy may be his inability to participate in such an intimate relationship. To effect a dialogue with the client, the therapist must accept and relate to the wholeness of the client, including the client's inability to enter into a dialogue. When she has accomplished this, the dialogue once again becomes a possibility. As the client's existence continues to unfold in his interactions with the therapist, and the therapist continues to embrace the client's wholeness in their interactions, there is a continuing possibility of the dialogue occurring.

In most instances of so-called dialogue the relating takes place within ourselves. The other is defined by our perceptions and related to as if he were no more than that. In such cases, we do not relate to the unique wholeness of the other since it is beyond the boundaries of ourselves and cannot be encompassed in our perceptions. An acceptance of the unique wholeness of the other is a prerequisite for the dialogue.

Case Example

So-called dialogues frequently occur in therapy. Recently, while I was engaged in marital counseling with a couple, the husband turned to his wife and addressed her in something like the following manner, which I have heard time and time again in marital counseling from both the husband and the wife:

> Vicki, I want to be very clear with you so that there is no misunderstanding between us. As I have always told you, I am number one in this relationship. You cannot have anyone or anything before me. I must be taken care of first and then you can take care of others. I come before the kids, your mother, or even yourself. Do you understand? My needs, my wants come first. I must always be first. When I come home, I expect you to come up to me and greet me. I want you to kiss me and ask me how my day went before you do anything else. After you have taken care of my needs, if there is any time left, you can do what you want, but not before. Do you understand? If you want a loving, caring relationship with me, this if the only way it can happen. It is the only way we can stay together. I must always be number one. My wants and needs must always come first.

George went through his routine, or something similar, each time he was asked to define what he wanted in his marital relationship. Needless to say, his wife was beside herself. When he was asked what he was willing to do for her in return for such attention, his response was the same one I have heard too often in marital counseling, "Doc, I'll be there for her. She will get whatever she needs so long as it does not interfere with her caring for me. I must be number one."

George's relationship with Vicki was limited to his percep-

tions of her function and he could not relate to her unique wholeness. He related to her as an object whose purpose was to fulfill his
needs. He was seemingly incapable of seeing her as a person in her
own right—as Thou in an I–Thou relationship. Yet, in his mind,
he thought he was having a dialogue with his wife.

In order for George to have a genuine dialogue with Vicki,
he must relate to her as a unique person. Throughout the lifetime
of his relationship with her, her uniqueness will constantly unfold
in his dialogues with her in special kinds of experiences—special
in that each dialogue is a one-time occurrence, never occurring
before nor ever occurring again. There is no way he can accommodate the experience of it in his existing cognitive structure. The
moment he feels he has discovered a way to sort it into identifiable
characteristics or traits that exist within Vicki, he is no longer relating to her but to his perception of her.

Buber contended that "the limits of the possibility of dialogue are the limits of awareness" (Buber, 1965b, p. 10). To open
a dialogue George must become aware of the presence of Vicki by
turning toward her in an open, direct, unmediated, unrestricted and
nonreflexive acceptance of her otherness. He must not attempt to
monitor, analyze, abstract, or conceptualize the impact of her otherness but accept it in its fullness in the hope that she will do the same
and thus generate a dialogue. It is in dialogue that George can
encounter the unique wholeness of Vicki. We cannot call George's
past interaction with his wife a dialogue.

In subsequent sessions, I attempted to engage Vicki in dialogue. At first she was reserved and held back, refusing to be open
and straightforward in her expressions. She later confided that she
had learned not to trust men. They always wanted something from
her. Each time I engaged her in conversation, I made every effort
to understand her. I told her that when I asked why, I really wanted
to know why and was not using it as a rhetorical gimmick. I told
her I was like a dressmaker trying to get the best fit I could of her
thoughts and feelings. I asked her to regard my inquiries as sincere
attempts on my part to understand exactly how she felt. As she
became convinced of my sincerity, she began to open up. Within a
few sessions she was chattering freely with me about her feelings

and desires for the relationship. From time to time, I was able to relate to her unique wholeness as a person.

As the dialogue unfolded between us, George watched in amazement. It was if he had never realized that his wife existed in a world different from his need of her. He began to listen with interest to our conversations. At times, we discussed him with respect to her feelings and reactions to him. I asked him, as part of his therapy, to listen and try to learn how his wife saw him. In subsequent sessions, he began to address her differently. He began to see that he could understand her point of view without giving up his own. This gave him the freedom to listen and inquire with more depth into her way of seeing things. Positive changes began to occur in their relationship. She reported that she was beginning to feel that there was hope for their marriage. George had become more considerate and, at times, was concerned about her wishes regarding certain matters. When I asked George why he had changed, he stated that he had begun to realize that Vicki had needs just as he did, and he should consider them.

Several sessions later they announced that they did not think they needed to come to therapy for a while since they were getting along better. They felt that they now had a way of talking to one another that helped each to understand what the other needed. They stated that although they could not explain it, something had happened. When pressed for a more explicit explanation they stated that they were able to communicate better. "George listens to me now" or "I now understand Vicki better."

Although these may seem to be plausible reasons to George and Vicki, something more profound had happened. Something had happened in the reality between them that changed their relationship. They had learned to engage in genuine dialogue. Since the between was not found in either George or Vicki, but in the interaction between them, its work was a mystery to them. While it was doing its healing work, neither of them was aware of its presence. They could consciously apprehend the healing achieved in the between—its effect, but not its process. When either reflected upon its presence, their observing self was no longer whole, and wholeness is a prerequisite for the presence of the between. The work of the between was accomplished in George and Vicki's prereflective activities. Only its achievements were accessible for reflection and contemplation.

Outcome Not Controlled by Therapist

For those therapists who must be able to explain and/or control the therapeutic process, this is not good news. The therapeutic dynamic comes in dialogue and remains a mystery. Its outcome is in the hands of neither the therapist nor the client. As therapists, we usually embrace a particular theoretical orientation in order to compensate for the mysterious work of the dialogue. It is our theoretical orientation (I–it relationships) that guides and directs most of our dealings with the client. At best, this orientation provides an organized structure through which we are able to interact with the unique wholeness of our client. At worst, it prevents us from making contact with the client's wholeness. Our theoretical orientation can only generate statements about certain aspects of the client that may be useful in directing him in the I–it world. We may calculate the client's typology, profile on a Minnesota Multiphasic Personality Inventory, configurations on the Rorschach, themes in a Thematic Apperception Test, or an axis in the American Psychiatric Association's most recent (1987) *Diagnostic and Statistical Manual* (DSM-III-R). We can do all these things and still fail to assess the client as a total person.

Although the dialogical psychotherapist may be hesitant to become a theoretical protagonist, she certainly is aware of the place of theory in the therapeutic process. The therapist's theoretical orientation anchors her in a reality seen through the framework of her theory, which she finds useful in alleviating the symptoms of the client. Yet it is often limited to those difficulties the theoretical approach is designed to deal with and cannot be effective in dealing with the unique wholeness of the client.

Summation and Preview

I once had a client return for his second session with me. He stated, "Before we begin our session today, I have something I want to say to you." For a moment I was panic stricken. He looked so very serious. I was certain I must have done something wrong in the first session. He proceeded, "As I was driving home after our last session,

I was so overcome with feelings that I had to pull off the road and weep. I have never felt like that before in my life and I have been in therapy before. After I got home, I had to tell my wife about it." I thought, "Oh God, here it comes I must have really screwed up the last time." In my mind it had been a rather mundane session of history taking except for several moments of closeness in which I had experienced the presence of the between. He continued, "It was the most wonderful feeling I have ever had. For the first time in my life someone really understood how I felt. That has never happened to me before. I could not let you start the session without expressing my appreciation for what you did." It was obvious that he felt something very significant had happened in those few moments of closeness that made it the most significant session in his therapeutic experience, and he felt it had originated in me. To the contrary, it did not come from me as the result of some special technique or unusual performance on my part. It was the result of our dialogue.

When I have sought a dialogue by struggling both to be present to the client and to make the client present, I have always encountered a kind of frustration which is disheartening. As I have learned to relax and allow my experience of the client in all of his mystery to come into my being without analysis or contemplation, something happens. The effect of this something is the work of the between and is felt in its subsequent moments. There has been a dialogue. It is in the fleeting moments, when therapist and client enter the between that the true work of healing is done. The remainder of the session is at best a repairing of various aspects of the self's existence but never the whole self. The dialogue is the expression within which the work of dialogical therapy is accomplished.

In the next chapter I will discuss our innate ability to distance ourselves from another and then to relate, that is, to recognize and hold ourselves apart from that which is not of us and in the process interact with it as a separate entity. This ability presents us with two ways of relating to the world, each of which has a profound impact on our development. It is this aspect of our nature—distancing and relating—that makes the dialogue possible as well as enables us to relate to the other as an object without regard for his unique wholeness.

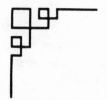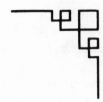

4

Distancing
and Relating

Our relationships allow us to move beyond our instinctual natures to those qualities that distinguish us as human beings. We see this in our ability to decide how we will relate to the world around us. Buber tells us that homo sapiens, unlike other species, were not content with just the perception of things and their conditions, and so they began to perceive their own perceiving (Buber, 1988, p. 49).

This apperceptive ability presents us with relational powers that, presumably, are not available to other species. Certainly they are not found in any species to the extent that they are found in humans.

For Buber, the ability to gain access to the unique wholeness of the other in our relationship is founded on a pair of ontological givens: distancing and relating. He contends that our innate ability to distance and relate provides the basis for our interactions with the world (Buber, 1988, pp. 10-11). The first of the pair, distancing, is a prerequisite for the second, relating. Distancing sets the other person apart from us, making it possible for us to experience his unified wholeness without fragmentation. In this way we can relate to all of the person and not just certain characteristics or traits. This experience of relating to the wholeness of the other results in the client's inner growth.

Thickening the Distance

When we do not use distance to hold the other apart as a being separate from us, something entirely different happens in our relating. We relate to the other as an object and not as unique whole. Buber has referred to this as "thickening the distance" (Buber, 1988, p. 12). What Buber meant is difficult to understand until we grasp the meaning of relating to the other as an object. The word *object* comes from the Latin word "ob-jectum," which means something thrown before, an obstacle to be conquered, manipulated, or transformed (Barrett, 1958, p. 232). The idea of conquering or manipulating characterizes an I-It relationship. We conquer, manipulate, or transform the other's unique wholeness by imposing our own categories on it. We do this as a conscious activity that never includes our whole self nor does it encompass the wholeness of the other.

When we thicken the distance, we experience the other as an accumulation of characteristics and/or traits that can be added to or subtracted from as we choose, depending on our inclination. The use of distancing determines the type of relationship we have with the other. When I use the distance to hold the other apart from myself as a separate being, there is the possibility of an I-Thou relationship. When I thicken the distance and relate to the other as selected traits, only an I-It relationship is possible.

I-It Relationships

The nature of I-Thou relationships was discussed in greater detail in the previous chapter; here we explore the nature of I-It relationships. Our discussion requires the unpacking or analyzing of Buber's philosophical anthropology—the twofold movement of distancing and relating. The explanation may be better understood by some readers if it is couched in psychological terms.

Psychologically speaking, our apperceptive ability makes it possible for us to have a relationship within ourselves—between our perceptions and our perceptions of our perceptions. This manner of relating does not require us to go out to meet the other. We can relate to the particular characteristics embodied in our perceptions of the other as opposed to relating directly to the other. In such cases, the nature of the interaction is determined by the particular perceptual characteristic that is our focal point. We may focus on the other's gender, his ethnicity, his vocation, his demeanor, or any characteristic we can perceive; our selection would be colored by our past experience, current mood, and prevalent need at that time.

In this type of relationship—when we select the particular characteristic of the other with which we wish to interact—the other becomes no more than our perceptions. Our interaction is not with the other but with our perception of his characteristics. In these cases we never relate to the wholeness of the other but only to parts of him. The other becomes the object of our perceptions.

Such interactions are not mutual but distinctively subject–object relationships. They are mediated and not direct. The relationship is mediated by our selective perception of the other. Presentness is "an elemental relationship which grasps the other without reduction or abstraction in all his concreteness" (Buber, 1988, p. 70). Presentness is not a characteristic of this type of relationship, which is not full and complete in itself but is a means to an end. The relationship is not by its nature intense. It is mundane and serves a function necessary to our ongoing existence as a creature in the world. Such relationships are rational and even in their more complicated forms can be understood from a psychological point of view; they are not ineffable.

Case Examples

This I-It manner of relating is usually the source of our client's illness even as our I-Thou relating is the source of his healing. When a person is constantly responded to as an object that possesses certain characteristics, he or she tends to reflect those characteristics. This reaction is illustrated in a twelve-year-old client I had. His father met me in the reception area and told me in his presence how clumsy the boy was. He was so intense in his description of Johnny's awkwardness that all I could think of was to get the boy away from him as soon as possible. As we were leaving, the father remarked that his son would spill the cup of hot chocolate he had in his hand before he had been in my office five minutes. The youngster protested but could not stifle his father's comments. Once in the office, I assured the boy that I knew he could handle his chocolate in spite of his father's prediction. He very carefully set the cup on the stand next to where he was seated. He looked at me with a sense of satisfaction and we began our discussion. Within five minutes he became excited about something he was discussing with me and began to gesture with wide sweeps of his arms. In the process he hit the cup of chocolate and splashed it over the wall. Clumsiness had become his way of being in the world. Johnny's behavior illustrates a self-fulfilling prophecy that results from the absence of dialogue. Because of his behavior, we may assume that his relationship with his father has been characteristic of an I–It nature, and his clumsiness is the consequence of his father's manner of relating to him. The father's perception that Johnny is clumsy is sufficient to limit Johnny's expression of himself. Johnny has lost touch with his ability to be graceful; it has been severed from his wholeness due to the lack of dialogue in his life. Thus Johnny fulfills his father's expectations of his clumsiness.

In another instance, I was seeing a beautiful young woman in her twenties. Her husband was the son of a prominent person in the community and she often found herself in the presence of what she called "the beautiful people." Her complaint was that they constantly made fun of her, hurting her deeply. When I asked what they said to her, she stated that they were always telling her how pretty she was and how much they admired her gracefulness. She was convinced they were lying to her. Near the end of one of the later sessions she directed a verbal tirade at me. She said, "You are no better than the rest. You pretend to be honest and then do the same things the others have done." When I asked what she meant, she told me how unkind I was and that as a professional, I should be ashamed of myself. I had treated her as if she were somebody when I knew she was nothing. Her distortion of her image before others was of psychotic proportions.

I later learned that when she was a child her father, who worked very unusual hours, would leave early in the morning and return about two hours before she came home from school. By that time her father and mother would be drunk on gin martinis and would proceed in their drunken stupor to berate her. As in the case of Johnny, this young woman was the victim of excessive I–It relating. Her early formative years were replete with such encounters with both her mother and father. They had imposed their own negative perceptions on her. In the absence of dialogue she was not able to be confirmed as anything other than what their constant abuse and belittling behavior had led her to believe she was. Consequently, she saw herself as a worthless, stupid blonde.

Another client illustrates how we may move beyond relating to someone as an it to interacting with the whole person. The client, Charley, stated that he had in the past felt cut off from his feelings. He had recently fallen in love with a woman who had aroused these old feelings of isolation and abandonment. He thought they had their origin in his early childhood experiences with his parents, both of whom were alcoholics. In the course of treatment, he told me how he had learned to turn off his feelings totally. He simply did whatever was necessary in relationships to make others happy without regard for his own needs. This behavior had been especially true in his previous marriage. He had gone along with whatever his wife had wanted regardless of how he felt. The only exception to his complete subservience to others was his job. He was an administrator with considerable responsibility involving the supervision of several hundred employees. There he was able to execute his responsibilities without regard for how others felt. It was the only part of his life in which he felt he was in control. On the job he simply followed policy without having to be concerned for how he or others felt.

In the course of Charley's treatment, at the insistence of his girlfriend, he began to explore and reclaim the feelings he had suppressed. From time to time, he began to experience his wholeness. It was one of these moments of wholeness that Charley shared with me in a later session. During the weekend prior to the session, he had met with a friend and had spent several hours with him mutually sharing their feelings. He spoke of the wonderful sensation he had experienced as a result of being able to be whole in his relationship with his friend. He had never before had such an experience. In the past, he had always been the supportive one for his friends and listened to them, but he had never shared himself with them. He stated that the way he related to them was to take them into himself. While this was occurring, he would often say to himself things like, "I don't need this bullshit. I'm just a garbage can for these people." These encounters had always been draining experiences for him. But the recent interaction with his friend was different. He had come away feeling energized, even though this friend had shared horrendous problems with him. It was such a moving experience that he felt it had affected the way he interacted with his employees. He was now much more concerned about determining who they were before he made decisions about how he would deal with them.

What Charley described was an experience in which he was able to move beyond an I-It way of relating to an I-Thou interaction. By restoring his wholeness, he was able to hold his friend apart from himself as a separate being and relate to his friend's unique wholeness. In other words, he did not bring his friend into himself and relate only to his perceptions of his friend's characteristics. He was able to exercise his ability to hold his distance and relate in a way that made it possible for him to interact with his friend in a special way—to go out and meet directly with his friend in all his wholeness without the benefit of a perceptual screen. Such an interaction always affects each of the partners in a positive fashion.

Previously when Charley was not able to experience his wholeness because of being cut off from certain feelings, it was impossible for him to relate to the wholeness of his friends. The I that Charley brought to the relationship with his friends, before the restoration of his wholeness, was capable only of relating to those negative traits that his friends brought to the interaction. He was not able to go outside of himself to meet them in all of their wholeness. He thickened the distance. This resulted in limiting the interaction to only the negative aspects they presented. He was unable to imagine the wonder of their wholeness that encompassed not only what they were now but also all that they could become. Inevitably, these were very draining experiences for Charley.

The two different ways of responding to distancing in our relating can be seen in two married couples who came to me for help. Both couples were in the process of separating. They were middle-aged and had grown children. The husband of the first couple asked that I meet with him and his wife to discuss their separation. He did not wish to enter marital counseling and expressed an emphatic desire for only counseling that would expedite the separation. He hoped his wife would continue to see me if she wished after they were separated. He indicated that he would be willing to attend as many sessions as was necessary for his wife to understand and accept his leaving her.

Each time we met, the husband would start the session by announcing his intention to leave the wife. The wife would then spend the rest of the session talking almost nonstop trying to convince him to stay. The husband would remain silent throughout most of the session with only an occasional response. He attempted to be as kind and supportive as possible but did not relent in his determination to leave her.

As the sessions progressed, it became increasingly obvious that the wife was unable to relate to her husband's request because she had thickened the distance in their relationship and could not see him as separate from her. She felt that all of her physical and psychological needs were met by him. Her personal and social identification were located in him. She felt that she had no existence apart from him. She stated that she loved him so much that she could not live without him. She became so desperate at the close of the session she begged him not to leave her. They left the office with her weeping on his shoulder.

The wife of this couple had used all her efforts to conquer, manipulate, or transform her husband so that he conformed to her perception of him as an object who functioned for her comfort. She could not distance from him and thus relate to him as a being separate from herself. She could not see him apart from her own desires. She was able to relate to him only as an object whose function was to fulfill her needs. There was a thickening of the distance that impaired her ability to relate to her husband's unique wholeness.

A week or so later the wife of the second couple appeared in my office asking if I would counsel her and her husband. She confided that she intended to leave him and wished to tell him in my presence. She indicated that there was no hope of her continuing in the marriage. I agreed to see her and her husband for the explicit purpose of her announcing her intent to separate from him. The next week she and her husband appeared at my office. Shortly after the session began, she turned to her husband and told him she wanted a divorce. She told him that she did not love him and had found someone else whom she did love and wished to marry this person as soon as possible. He was stunned by her announcement. He sat silently for a few moments struggling to maintain his composure as he wept quietly. The tears rolled down his cheeks as he spoke to his wife of his feelings for her. He looked into his wife's face and said, "It breaks my heart to lose you, but if you have found someone else with whom you can be happier, I will not try to stop you. I love you too much ever to stand in the way of your happiness." In that moment, I was ashamed of my own shallowness as I witnessed the depth of this man's love. He embraced his wife, still weeping, and left the session with her following. He was capable of seeing his wife's needs and desires apart from his own. There was distancing and relating in his interaction with his wife.

In view of the immaturity displayed in I-It relationships, we might assume that developmentally this relational ability precedes I-Thou relationships. However, Friedman tells us that Buber contends this is not true (Buber, 1988, pp. 12-13). Buber saw distancing and relating as complementary polarities, and in our early development they are first experienced together in I-Thou relationships. "The baby does not proceed directly from complete unity with its mother to the primary I-Thou relation" (Buber, 1988, p. 13). However, the child from its first days has the ability to sense other beings as different from himself and thus enter into an I-Thou relationship. It is later that the baby learns to thicken the distance and relate to the mother as an object and enter into an I-It relationship with her. Buber does not describe these stages of development other than to tell us they occur in our infancy. Hycner informs us in the seventh chapter of his proposed book, *Dialogical Psychotherapy and Intersubjectivity Theory: A Bridge Between,* that we must remember Buber was first a philosopher and the manner in which he presents his philosophical anthropology is not as a psychologist. A psychological description of our early childhood development from the dialogical perspective has yet to be accomplished.

Summation and Preview

The two different ways of relating, I–Thou and I–It, which distancing and relating make possible, are crucial to the practice of dialogical psychotherapy. An understanding of the client's pathology often may be traced to events in his or her life that have interfered with the appropriate utilization of these two polarities, distancing and relating.

In the following chapter the reader will see how healing occurs in the meeting as a result of the dialogue; the therapist and the client distance from each other and then relate in an I–Thou encounter. It is in this relating that the meeting takes place in which healing occurs. Healing is not found in something the therapist does to the client nor something the client does to himself; it is found in the meeting.

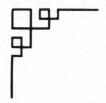

5

Healing
Through Meeting

The purpose of dialogical psychotherapy is to effect a healing of our relational self. Buber has contended that this healing takes place in a special kind of meeting of the therapist with the client. The previously described elements (the between, the dialogical, and distancing and relating) can be seen as converging upon this concern, healing through meeting. The meeting is nestled in the I–Thou relationship seen in the dialogue. The healing occurs in those moments when the therapist and the client mutually turn with their whole being and relate, thus creating a new reality between them. It is in this meeting that healing takes place.

The Nature of Dialogical Healing

Buber contended that the healing of the personal self, whether it is labeled integration, maturing, self-actualization, individuation, or whatever, is the result of what takes place in the meeting and is not a self-initiated or a self-imposed process (Buber, 1957, p. 97; 1958, p. 132-133). The meeting takes the client beyond his fragmented and conflicted self to a grasp of his whole being. Mysterious as this may be to the client, he experiences it as healing; the self is never sick alone but always in a situation between it and other existing beings (Buber, 1967, p. 142). Thus, the healing through meeting comes when it is central and not ancillary in dialogical psychotherapy (Friedman, 1985, chap. 1).

To the average person, healing usually means curing something that is wrong with us. If I asked such a person how this occurs, he or she might say that it depends on what needs to be healed. If the ailment is physical, we go to a physician. If it is emotional and/or mental, we go to a psychologist. If it is spiritual, we go to a clergyman. Each of the disciplines represented by these individuals has its own special method of repairing what is wrong. In this hypothetical discussion, we have been told that healing involves, first, curing something that needs to be cured; second, a method used to accomplish the curing; and third, an agent who applies the method for curing.

Healing from the dialogical perspective is to make the client whole. The method is the therapeutic dialogue as it is initiated by the therapist and responded to by the client. However, to understand truly what is meant by healing, we must be aware of what is wrong with the client who comes for help. He presents himself as disjointed and conflicted in his efforts to cope with the world. For example, he may be disjointed in the sense that he constantly brings inappropriate and negative feelings to new situations because of their perceived similarity to old situations in which he has been treated badly. He may be rigid and inflexible because of trying to cope with the demands of his day-to-day existence in a manner that is commensurate with a way of being that has been imposed on him. He is conflicted in that he is unable to utilize his capabilities for adjustment because of conflicts with other of his abilities (for example, the ambivalence of love-hate or of his relation to authority). It is in this sense that the client's self is fragmented. Yet the dialogical psychotherapist contends that in the client there exists the capability of coping effectively if only the client were able to utilize all of his abilities by eliminating his fragmentation. It is not the case that the client can only be the way he is, divided and conflicted.

He is capable of adjustment if he has access to all his possibilities, that is, his wholeness.

Healing by Synthesis

The method used to heal the fragmented self is psychosynthesis and not analysis. The healing process does not involve breaking the self down into its fundamental elements and separating them out for purposes of treatment. Instead it brings the elements of the self together so that they function as a coordinated or harmonious whole. This is accomplished by the therapist bringing her own unified wholeness to the meeting. In doing so, she provides a container for the client's shattered self while provoking, arousing, and demanding its crystallization. She is present to the client in the fullness of her being without pretense or sham. She does not foster dependence on the part of client by suggesting or manipulating the outcome. She faces the client without any preconceptions. She does not offer suggestions of how the client should be, but provides him an image that "lets him look through . . . [her] . . . as through a glass, into being and now [lets him] discover being in itself . . . empowered as the core of living unity" (Buber, 1960, p. 132). The attitude and demeanor of the therapist in the healing meeting with the client is discussed in much more detail in Chapter Fourteen.

Case Examples

An example of healing through meeting is my work with Geraldine. A woman in her thirties, she appeared in my office and asked that I help her to find her way in life. As a child she had been sexually abused by her father and psychologically abused by her mother. She had recently returned from another city to which she had fled while suffering from a dissociative disorder. Her flight had been precipitated by her mother's continuing abuse. She stated she had been nothing but a victim and did not know how to take care of herself. In one of the later sessions I confronted Geraldine with her assessment of herself. "You insist that you only know how to be taken care of. You have told me that your mother would be glad to take you back and take care of you. If that is all you can be, why do you not go back to her and allow yourself to be taken care of?'' She screamed out, ''I could not stand to be treated that way by my mother again!'' It was at this point in our dialogue that I was able to point out to her that in the wholeness of her being she was much more than someone who had to be taken care of. Her mother's treatment of her had resulted in her focusing on only one aspect of her existence, thereby fragmenting her wholeness and severing all that she could be—except someone to be taken care of—from her imagination. Our dialogue had resulted in her recapturing in her imagination her wholeness, with all of its potential for her to become a self-sufficient person.

As Geraldine grasped the potential of her wholeness, she became frightened. She protested she did not know whether she would be able to withstand the fear she felt as she allowed herself to imagine what she could do with her life. This is not uncommon in clients who have been the victims of prolonged I-It relationships that have resulted in their being cut off from the potential that exists in the wholeness of their being. It was a potential that Geraldine had not been able to imagine until our meeting. She explained that confronting it made her feel as though she was about to step out into utter darkness, and that once she did there would be no bottom; she would fall forever. I assured her that I would stay with her in her fear and that it was the only way she could experience that possibility that had been severed from her imagination as a result of her interactions with her mother.

At some point in our interaction, the healing had begun. Within a few sessions Geraldine began speaking of her plans to begin a new career. She presented herself with a clarity and confidence that had not been present before our dialogue. That part that had been separated from her unified wholeness—her ability to feel adequate—was in the process of being retrieved. Within a few sessions she began looking for employment that was commensurate with her newfound confidence.

Often the client's healing involves the courage to act on what he already knows he is. I once saw a client who illustrates what happens when we are too frightened to respond to what we are uniquely intended to be. Mark was a widower in his fifties who had lost his wife ten years earlier. After her death he had refused to mourn and had become what he described as quietly angry, resentful, and fearful. He presented the symptoms of an avoidant personality disorder. He had cut himself off from all meaningful contact with others. Although he lived with his daughter, he refused to relate to her. He had minimal contact with the world. He seldom went out of the house and had no special activities. On his job he put out the least amount of effort necessary to hold the position. He stated that he was constantly afraid of being fired. He would not prepare meals for himself although he was a good cook. He lived on junk food and had a serious weight problem. For several years he had not filed his income tax return. He reported that he was extremely depressed, and I referred him to a psychiatrist for medication.

As the treatment progressed, I spoke to Mark about his not responding to what he was intended to be. I told him he had been unfaithful to himself and he knew it, and he had avoided doing anything about it. I asked him to confront the Internal Revenue Service (IRS) matter—to stop avoiding the issue and deal with it like the person he knew he was. I explained to him that deep within himself he had always known what he was supposed to do but had avoided it. This discussion was prompted by our previous dialogues in which I had come very close to him, and I was not as presumptuous as I may appear in my description of the event. I had learned to care for this lonely man and had become very concerned for him. According to him, I was the only meaningful contact he had with anyone.

It was then that Mark told me he had used his depression to escape from doing the things he knew he should be doing. As a result of our interaction, he found the courage to contact the IRS and is now in the process of dealing with what he has neglected for over five years. He told me how frightened he was but somehow as a result of our interaction he had found the courage to face his fear. It is difficult to appreciate what a remarkable feat this has been for him without knowing of his prolonged withdrawal from the world. His newfound sense of being is reflected in his renewed interest in the world around him.

Our theoretical assumptions may entice us into a meeting in which the unique wholeness of the client is not encountered, thus precluding healing from occurring. As therapists, we often delude ourselves into believing that we are meeting with our client when in actuality we are meeting with our theoretical perceptions of the client. I have unknowingly been the perpetrator of such a meeting, with a client named Aaron.

Aaron lived alone and had never been married. He was referred for reasons that were never clear. I was told that he was schizotypal and was in need of professional help. I consulted my DSM-III-R (American Psychiatric Association, 1987) for the symptoms of such a person and awaited his arrival at the office. Throughout the first session I observed him closely, looking for the nine symptoms of a schizotypal personality disorder. By the conclusion of the first session, I had found five of the nine symptoms necessary for a diagnosis of this disorder.

Throughout the session, Aaron was ill at ease in my presence, indicating extreme discomfort in social situations involving unfamiliar people. He displayed odd or eccentric behavior. He was unkempt and mumbled to himself off and on during the session. He described himself as an odd-shaped screwball. His hair was uncombed, his shoulders were narrower than his hips, and his clothes were rumpled as if he had been sleeping in them. He stated that he had no close friends and had never had a girlfriend in his life. So far his history was not unlike that of most of the other clients with schizotypal personality disorders I had seen. He rarely responded with appropriate gestures, smiles, or nods. His speech was impoverished and, at times, vague and inappropriately abstract. He was suspicious of his supervisor and felt the man was trying to fire him for no good reason. Once again, this view of the world was similar to that of other schizotypals I had seen. He indicated during the interview that he had always been considered odd since his high school days. He presented a pervasive pattern of deficiencies in his interpersonal relations and displayed peculiarities in his ideation, appearance, and behavior. No doubt about it, Aaron was schizotypal.

At the conclusion of the session I was convinced that an appropriate diagnosis had been made and that I now knew enough about Aaron to develop a treatment plan for him. I deluded myself into believing I could capture the essence of his being in the diagnosis. I harbored vague notions of a person who was lost in his own world with very little concern for others, a person who avoided the responsibility of real contact with others because he did not like people. I am ashamed to admit the cavalier attitude with which I had approached Aaron's treatment.

In the initial course of treatment, I constantly felt cut off from him. No matter how hard I tried he was not accessible. I consoled myself that this was further proof of his disorder. You cannot expect to make meaningful contact with these kinds of people. In the midst of my ineptness, I began to realize that I was not seeking a meeting with the real person sitting before me but a hypothetical person derived from my abstractions and generalities. I had been trying to meet with a person who did not exist except in my mind and the DSM-III-R category. It was at this point that significant changes occurred in my interactions with Aaron.

In the sessions that followed I came to know Aaron as a person who was entirely different from the one I had conjured up on the basis of my diagnosis. As I became more attuned and responsive to his way of being, he expressed concern about my way of doing therapy with him. He suggested that I offer him more constructive criticism. He asked that my feedback to him be more realistic even if it meant disagreeing with him. I struggled to comply with his requests.

As Aaron's trust in me grew, he began to reveal his secret thoughts and feelings. He shared his fear of people. People had always made fun of him and played jokes on him because he was different. He told how he had been the butt of the jokes of the guys at work. Although they had said they were his friends, they had constantly made fun of him. He stated, "All I had wanted was friends, but you cannot trust people." He then burst out in a tirade: "I want to see someone rip out their guts. I want someone to burn them up and I will watch them writhe in pain. I want them caught in an earthquake that scares them to death for what they did to me." Aaron's hurt swept over me in that moment as I watched a small boy with dry eyes struggle with his pain. It was as if he had been hurt so much that he was beyond tears.

In a later session he told me how lonely he was. He had invited people to his home and spent money on food, but no one came. They had all promised they would come, but they didn't. He told me how hard he had tried to meet a girl, all to no avail. At another time, he confided that he had never had sex and longed for someone with whom he could have a relationship. Both of his parents were dead and his older brother would have nothing to do with him. He had learned that others cannot be trusted, not even your own family members. You must watch them or they will hurt you. His only protection from the pain of rejection was to remain aloof, no matter how lonely he felt.

Finally, Aaron decided it was time to test our relationship. He came into the meeting late. I expressed concern about his tardiness. At this point he exploded. "You are no different from the others. You treat me with total disregard. On several occasions you have ignored me when I have been talking to you and I am tired of being treated like I am of no consequence." I thought, here is proof of the diagnosis—this is the way you would expect a schizotypal to react. However, he was right about my ignoring him. I met with a very disturbed client before his session and often had trouble getting myself together before seeing him. I apologized to him and promised to not let it happen again.

It was then that something happened to me that I had not anticipated. It was as if the wholeness of my being screamed out for a meeting with the Aaron I had come to know and not a schizotypal personality disorder. I turned to Aaron and spoke directly to him: "Aaron, I have come to care for you and I am not going to have you think otherwise. For the first time in your life you have met a person who is not going to be goaded into rejecting you no matter how mean you are to me. I care about you and what happens to you."

The sincerity of my concern seemed to immobilize him momentarily. He sat silently as if trying to assimilate what I had said. He worked his lips back and forth as I had learned he did when he was upset. At first I thought he would bolt from the room, but he did not. He leaned back in his chair with a faint smile. It was the first time he had shown any sign of happiness. I felt an overpowering sense of compassion for him in that moment and he was aware of my regard. At last there had been a meeting with the unique wholeness of my client. In subsequent sessions, I was attentive and saw the healing that came from our meeting. Aaron was never again with me the tormented man who had first sought my help.

The last time I saw Aaron was when he dropped by the office to tell me, with pride, how he was managing to straighten out his life. He stood staring at the office wall as I told him how proud I was of him. For an instant the wry smile appeared and his mouth began to make movements like someone savoring a tasty morsel of food. He mumbled something to himself, shook my hand, and left the office. I was deeply touched by our meeting and I am convinced he was also.

Summation and Preview

The implications of this element, healing through meeting, have a profound and extensive impact on the focus of dialogical psycho-therapy. Healing is not found in something the therapist does to the client with his skill and technique. The healing results from the meeting with the client. In the next chapter I will discuss the results of this healing. It always produces a movement in the client—a movement that expresses his or her uniqueness. It is in this move-ment that the individual's personal direction emerges. It arises in the meeting, and it is in the meeting that the client is empowered to pursue it.

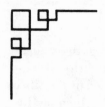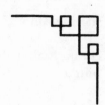

6

Personal
Direction

Dialogical psychotherapy is primarily interested in the client's on-going, unfolding direction as a person. Buber defines our direction as the unique contribution that only we and no other can make to the world. It is not predetermined but discovered ever anew in each unique, concrete event. Finding our direction involves the ability to confront our potential and decide our course of action without asking anything other than what is right and what is wrong in that situation. It is our awareness of what we are "in truth," of what in our unique and unrepeatable existence we are intended to be. From this awareness, when it is fully present, the comparison with what we actually are and what we are intended to be can emerge (Buber, 1952, pp. 95-96; Friedman, 1960, pp. 95-97).

Uniqueness of Personal Direction

The dialogical psychotherapist does not claim that the pursuit of the client's personal direction moves him toward a common implicit or explicit goal for which all clients must strive. The client's personal direction is suitable only for him, the one for whom it is personal. What a client is directed toward and the path he takes to reach it is peculiar to him.

The thrust of the client's personal direction is the expression of his uniqueness, which emerges from his unified wholeness. His direction does not arise within him as the result of self-realization— an introspective process—as he looks inward and ponders. It arises and unfolds between him and the therapist. Unfolds in the sense that it is always contingent on the outcome of his interaction with the world and is not subject to a predetermined course. Its goal is not some preconceived notion conjured up by himself or others, family, therapist, or society. It has no preconceived outcome but the fulfillment of the client's uniqueness. Its course remains a mystery until it unfolds in the meeting.

It is the absence of direction in the client's life that has contributed to his disturbance. He has either sought to live a life that is familiar and predictable and found it impossible to tolerate, or he has demanded a world that is certain and predictable and found it impossible to achieve. The resolution of the client's disturbance lies in his pursuit of his personal direction that takes him beyond his demands for these characteristics in his ordinary, everyday experiences.

The pursuit of the client's personal direction generates movement in his life along a path of development that for most clients is uncomfortable, to say the least, and for many is excruciatingly difficult. The client's pursuit forces him to struggle with the realization of his uniqueness. There are no familiar landmarks to guide him, for he has never been this way before. The usual and the predictable are not available. His past ways of conducting himself are not appropriate. He must respond as if each moment were an end in itself, hoping that his response will be followed by another such moment and yet another and another as he moves towards the fulfillment of his uniqueness.

The dialogical psychotherapist feels that in spite of the distressing feelings that often accompany the demands of the client's pursuit of his personal direction, it is necessary if the client is to recover. His direction is found in the realm of the between, where the uniqueness of his unified wholeness is encountered and he is endowed with the imagination to pursue it.

Genesis of Personal Direction

Our personal direction is not found in the summation of what we and the other bring to the meeting. It is found in the new reality which our meeting generates. Buber speaks of the color red not being found in either the things or the soul (psyche). A red-receiving eye and a red-engendering oscillation produce a phenomenon, red. He asks the question, "How could we in our thinking place together these worlds so divorced from one another?" (Buber, 1952, p. 5). However, it is in this third world—the phenomenon produced by the meeting—that our personal direction is found.

If this were all that came out of the meeting, it would be asinine to expect the client to pursue the prompting of such a strange and alien reality. He has no way of accommodating it in his cognitive structure, for it speaks to the wholeness of his being. But as a result of the meeting his wholeness has been unified and he is empowered to receive and pursue the direction found in the meeting. Also, the therapist, who has brought his wholeness to the meeting, is empowered to support the client in his pursuit. Both the elements of inclusion and confirmation are involved in this endeavor of the therapist and will be discussed in subsequent chapters.

Foundation of Personal Direction

We cannot embrace personal direction as an element in dialogical psychotherapy without an understanding and acceptance of the following presuppositions:

1. Each client possesses a unique multiplicity of possibilities for being.
2. The actualization of these inner possibilities is called out in every encounter with each specific, concrete event in the world throughout the course of the client's lifetime.
3. Such encounters may appear to be randomized givens in the client's existence; however, to the extent that he responds to

each concrete event with his unique, unified personal wholeness, there is meaning and purpose in his life.
4. The client cannot attain the unity of his wholeness within himself. It is found in his interaction with another Thou.
5. It is in ever-renewing dialogue that the client's personal direction emerges, along with his empowerment to pursue it.
6. The client's experience of his personal direction may present
   him with a knowing that is not always amenable to his rational
   analysis.
7. To the extent that there is an absence of unity in the client's
   personal wholeness, there is fragmentation resulting in inner
   conflict and loss of direction. When this loss occurs, various
   defenses are brought into play by the disturbed client. At the
   very core of these defenses is a self-defeating attempt to effect
   healing without dialogue.

The client's pursuit of his personal direction involves his
willingness to confront an event and struggle to determine what is
right and what is wrong for him in that situation. The therapist
must be willing to stand with the client in his struggle. This involves being with the client as he allows the situation to call out
from the wholeness of his being that potential for responding that
is commensurate with his uniqueness. It is in the dialogue that the
personal direction of the client emerges.

The client's personal direction appears in the discovery and
actualization of his response to that situation. However, the client
is unable to apprehend and actualize the appropriate response
within himself. Both the discovery and power to execute his response comes from a reality that is beyond him—a reality that lies
between him and the other in dialogue. The client cannot find his
personal direction when he seeks it as a solitary endeavor outside
of dialogue. It does not come from within himself but from the
reality that is between himself and the other. The pursuit of his
personal direction outside of dialogue is futile.

Case Examples

The source of many of our clients' disturbances resides in their
secrets, which interfere with the pursuit of their personal direc-

tion—those issues with their accompanying feeling they have never dared share with others, which they have never explored in dialogue. A woman once came to share such a secret with me. She was married and had several children. She had been married most of her adult life. After she had seated herself on the couch before me, she blurted out her secret. "Doctor Heard, I know you are going to think I am crazy, but I want to have an affair with another man so bad I can hardly stand it. I have only been with my husband. When I married him I was a virgin, and I have never been with anyone else. I am dying to find out what it would be like to have sex with another man."

For a moment, I sat stunned. This was the last thing I expected to hear from her. After regaining my composure, I decided to take a supportive stance in order to create an ambiance in which she could feel free to explore her dilemma. I asked her why this presented a problem to her. After all, she was an attractive woman and certainly would have no problem finding a willing partner for her affair. In an attempt to stifle her desire, she stated that she loved her husband very dearly and could not stand the thought of hurting him. Besides, he was a good sex partner and it was not his fault that his wife wanted to find out what it would be like to have sex with a different man. I continued in my supportive stance and asked her why her husband should be involved. After all, she did not have to let him know. She stated that although he might not know, she would, and she did not think she could stand the guilt. It was something she just could not bring herself to do no matter how badly she wanted to. She continued by explaining how incompatible her desire was with her values. It was against everything she valued. It was adultery. No, she could not do it even though she wanted to very badly. It just was not in her to do something that was so contrary to her love for her husband and her values.

After she had completed her struggle and decided it was something she could not do, I complimented her on her stand. I spoke to her of my admiration for her—to want so much to do something and not do it because of her love for her husband and her values. It really said something about her as a person. I told her that I thought she was one heck of a woman. At this point she began to weep and ask how I could say something like that about her. If she had been the kind of woman I thought she was she would never have wanted to do such a thing. I responded to her protestations by telling her that it was the fact that she wanted so badly to do it and did not do it that determined the depth of her love for her husband and the strength of her values. Once again she protested that if she had really loved her husband enough she would never have wanted to experiment sexually in the first place.

In our ensuing discussions, she was able to differentiate between her desire and her culpability. She was able to see that her desire for an affair was certainly a part of her, but something less than her wholeness to which it belonged. By accepting and relating to her desire in the context of her unified wholeness, she prevented further fragmentation of her self. She was able in our interaction to realize that she was much more than her desire to have an affair. Her personal direction came in her decision to remain true to her husband and her values—a task that was inconceivable for her alone without lingering guilt and further fragmentation of herself. By embracing her wholeness in our interaction, we had created a reality that enabled her to seek out the appropriate response and be empowered to pursue it—her personal direction in that situation.

There are times when as a result of the dialogue the therapist is called on to take a more definitive stand with respect to the client's personal direction. This occurred in a session in which I was treating a young man who was suffering from gender dysphoria. I had been seeing him for several months and had listened patiently as he had presented a history I had heard often during the many years I had been seeing transsexual clients.

Eric had been married but was recently divorced because of his gender dysphoria. He was extremely depressed and felt he would be better off dead. He stated he was one of nature's freaks and did not deserve to live. He could not throw off the feeling that he was a female trapped in a male body. He had secretly felt this way as long as he could remember. Lately, these feelings were so strong that he stated he could not continue as a male unless he got some relief. He had attempted suicide but had been rescued by his friends.

As Eric continued to lament his lot in life, I grew increasingly impatient. It was in one of these moments that I felt Eric's deep disrespect for himself. The feeling swept over me. In response to it, I faced Eric and addressed him in anger. "I will not sit here any longer and listen to you demean yourself. I have come to respect and care for you and do not believe you are a freak of nature. You are part of nature's plan. People with your feelings appear with predictable frequency time and time again. Out of every 100,000 persons born, four of them have your dilemma. You are rare and in that sense valuable. I know you did not ask to be a gender dysphoric, but you are, and I believe whoever created us expects you to deal with it in the best way possible and that does not mean being disrespectful of yourself. Unless you can learn to respect your gender dysphoria, I do not wish to treat you any longer."

Needless to say Eric was shocked. He seemed genuinely impressed by my outburst. There was a decided change. From that point on in our interactions he seemed to sense my regard for the wholeness of his being, including his gender dysphoria. At the present time, he has almost completed his pre-surgical treatment requirement and is looking forward to sexual reassignment surgery, which is the alternative he has chosen. He is no longer a male, but a female in pursuit of her personal direction—striving to become all that her uniqueness calls her to be as a female.

Summation and Preview

Although the client's discovery and pursuit of his personal direction is most relevant to changes that occur in his life as a result of therapy, it is one of the most difficult elements to grasp. The client's unique potential, which appears in his response to the dialogue, is often manifested in ways that are unexpected and surprising to both the therapist and the client. It is not uncommon for the therapeutic encounter to evoke a direction in the client's life that does not logically follow from the content of the dialogue. From a rational point of view it is incomprehensible. However, we must remember that the client's personal direction speaks to his unique wholeness and not to those aspects of his existence that may be the focus of the therapist's concern.

The personal direction of the client's life is ongoing and unfolds again and again in the dialogue. Although it cannot be directed or ascertained by the therapist, the therapist must respect its presence and provide a setting that facilitates the client's finding it in the dialogue between them, for the between is the dynamic of dialogical psychotherapy. The dialogue is the method, and the client's discovery and pursuit of his personal direction is the therapeutic outcome and the focus of the dialogical psychotherapist's concerns. The restoration of our wholeness always produces a movement. It is in the direction of this movement that we find the purpose and meaning for our lives. Because of its importance, personal direction will again be addressed from time to time with reference to its presence in other elements of dialogical psychotherapy.

In the next chapter we will discuss that aspect of our existence that is pre-dialogical in that it is not available to us before the dialogue occurs. It is our potential for being that is called out from our personal wholeness by the meeting. It is also our potential for being that has been severed from our personal wholeness by our interactions with others in which there was no dialogue or the dialogue was aborted. It is our unconscious.

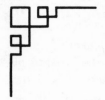

7

The
Unconscious

Each of us is a unique creation who cannot be divided into parts. Such a division takes away our unified wholeness. Yet for purposes of clarity, we can speak of our functions. In this section I will discuss our unconscious functions. Buber was still in the process of formulating his understanding of the unconscious at the time of his death; thus, the assumptions made regarding its implications for dialogical psychotherapy are more speculative than in the case of the other elements.

My discussion of our unconscious functions is not intended to be definitive. I have attempted to present a framework within which the dialogical psychotherapist may operate. The understanding of our unconscious functions is being formulated by a group who identify themselves as dialogical psychotherapists: Maurice Friedman, James De Leo, Richard Hycner, and William G. Heard.

Functions of the Unconscious

Buber thought of our unconscious as functioning in at least three different ways. First, he spoke of our unconscious as synonymous with our personal wholeness (Buber, 1967, pp. 155ff.; Friedman, 1985, pp. 143–145). Second, he saw it as the guardian of our personal wholeness (Friedman, 1985, p. 147); third, he agreed with Trüb who spoke of the unconscious as our psychic activities that have been fragmented and severed from the expression of our unified wholeness as a result of aborted or unfulfilled dialogues, that is, saying "no" to the meeting (Trüb, 1952, pp. 96, 98, 103; Friedman, 1991, p. 504). In this section we will explore these three ways of viewing our unconscious functions and their implications for the practice of dialogical psychotherapy.

Unconscious as Personal Wholeness

When Buber equated our unconscious with our personal wholeness, he contended that our unconscious is the ground of our being before it is split into its psychic and physical manifestations. It encompasses what we are and what we are intended to become—our uniqueness. All our possibilities of being, which are necessary for the fulfillment of our uniqueness, abide in our wholeness (unconscious) as potentials, devoid of the dimensions of time and space. Since we are finite creatures existing in a temporal and physical world, the apprehension of our unique potential requires that it be dissociated from our wholeness and these dimensions be imposed on it. This is accomplished by splitting the uniqueness into its psychic (inner) and physical (outer) manifestations—the psychic requiring the dimension of time only and the physical requiring the dimension of both time and space. When this split has been accomplished, it is possible for us to apprehend and actualize our unique potential in our phenomenological world.

Wholeness Actualized in the Between

Because of its unique nature, our wholeness can be apprehended only in that moment when we respond to a concrete event in our life with our whole being. At that moment, a new reality is generated between us and the other. It is only in this reality, the between, that we find the ability to actualize the appropriate potential of our wholeness—appropriate in the sense that it is the only fitting expression of our uniqueness in that situation. There is no way to contemplate or anticipate what will be called forth from our wholeness. Each concrete event and our response to it are unique, never having occurred before nor ever occurring again. We are responsible for responding in that situation with our whole self.

In order to respond with our whole self, we must be willing to tolerate the anxiety associated with the mystery of what awaits us in that encounter. Many of us are not willing to chance the ever-new present that comes to meet us in each situation. We attempt to protect ourselves from the uncertainty by seeking causality and order, orienting and securing ourselves from the unknown by generating a sense of predictability. We accomplish this by ignoring the uniqueness of the situation and responding to its abstractions and generalities rather than its wholeness. In such cases, we *have* an experience as opposed to *going out to* an experience. That is, we impose upon the experience its commonalities with other experiences rather than being changed by its uniqueness.

Growth Required for Wholeness

To the extent that we respond to each event with our whole selves we live an authentic life, realizing that to grow we must perpetually begin anew, perpetually risk all; our growth is not a once-and-for-all attaining but a continual becoming. The unresponsive person wants security once and for all. He wants a solid general truth that will not overturn him so he can remain static. We can see why the dialogue is so fleeting. True dialogue comes and goes, as by existential grace, as each partner is tempted to revert to the certainty and control that comes in the relative comfort of orienting himself in I-It relationships. The unresponsive person is not willing to pursue the personal direction of his life by facing the ever-new mystery awaiting him in each new situation. (The thoughts in this paragraph and the previous one are based on Buber's concepts of realization and orientation as presented in the first, second, and third chapters of his book, *Daniel: Dialogues on Realization*, 1965a).

Case Examples

When confronted with an unresponsive client the therapist can only stand with him and seek a dialogue. Clients are often capable of remarkable behavior in such situations. I once worked with a married woman who was a very helpless and dependent person. Her first response to any situation requiring her involvement was "I can't do it," no matter how simple the task. Consequently, her husband looked after her and took care of the day-to-day business of the family. She cooked, kept house, and played with her two sons. This was the extent of her activities.

The occasion for my seeing her was the recent paralysis of her husband's legs as the result of an automobile accident. She felt there was no way she could maintain the household and take care of the family. She wept and screamed while protesting her situation. It was impossible to contain her. She screamed out again and again, "Oh, my God! My God! My God! What am I going to do?" I did not know how to calm her. I attempted to be with her in her desperation and console her to the best of my ability. The weeping and wailing went on and on. "What am I to do? Doctor, why has this happened to us?" I was so caught up in her sense of helplessness that I also began to panic. She had convinced me as well as herself that there was really no way she could handle the situation. It was then I thought of the ontology of her personal wholeness. Although the parts of her wholeness with which she was responding were very expressive, they were not effective. Certainly she was not responding to the event with the wholeness of her being.

She continued to present herself as a frightened, helpless victim. I reminded myself that the person before me was much more than she was presenting at that moment. I struggled in my interactions with her to move beyond her limited perceptions of herself to grasp the unseen potential that resided in her personal wholeness. I was touched by her fear and sense of helplessness but at the same time convinced of her ability to cope with the demands of the situation. It was in this context that the dialogue occurred. "Mrs. Jackson, you are being called upon to do something you have never done before. You did not want to be placed in this situation, but you are. You must now pull from within yourself whatever it takes to get the job done. Whatever it takes resides within you, and you must bring it forth." At that moment I was absolutely convinced that she was able to do what had to be done to care for her family. I could detect a glimmer of hope in her voice as she replied, "I'll try Doctor, I'll try." The hysterical behavior disappeared and she appeared to experience herself in a much more confident manner. Sometime later my secretary called me at home to inform me of a call from Mrs. Jackson. My secretary was amazed at the difference in her. She asked, "What happened to that woman? She is so different. She seems to have gotten it together." During the weeks that followed, Mrs. Jackson continued to struggle with her sense of ineptness, but she did what needed to be done. She had been empowered to actualize the potential that resided in her personal wholeness.

The ontology of Mrs. Jackson's personal wholeness (unconscious) presented me, as her therapist, with a humbling experience. What happened with her was not under my control nor could it be accomplished by any technique or skill I possessed. As her therapist, I could only in my imagination be aware of her unique potential for dealing with the situation and await its empowerment in our dialogue. Its occurrence came by existential grace from what had been created between us in our meeting.

Unconscious as Guardian of Wholeness

Buber considered our unconscious not only synonymous with our personal wholeness but also its guardian. Because of our nature, even if we could bring our apperceptive abilities (conscious awareness) to bear upon our wholeness, there would be no phenomenon to apperceive prior to our expression of it. Apperception is not possible until an event calls out the potential from our wholeness for actualization. Only when this event occurs is the potential for responding dissociated from our wholeness and split into its psychic and physical manifestations—the required precursors for its phenomenological occurrence. It is then shaped and elaborated by us for expression. The moment we reflect upon our expression of our wholeness we are no longer whole. In that moment we become less than whole— fragmented—because a part of us has been severed from our unified wholeness to reflect.

The ontology of the unconscious has profound implications for dialogical psychotherapists. Because of its nature, the client's wholeness (unconscious) cannot be directly accessed by analysis.

There is no dialectical technique capable of apprehending it. The client's unique potential for being in each situation is protected from the therapist's intrusiveness and remains a mystery even to the client himself. However, Buber does acknowledge that it is possible for the therapist to have a substantial effect upon the way in which the client shapes and elaborates what which is dissociated from his wholeness, such as memory of past events and recollection of dreams, but no one, not even the client, can have direct access to it (Friedman, 1985, p. 146).

Unconscious and Fragmentation of Our Wholeness

Farber felt that Buber used the term unconscious in two different ways (Friedman, 1985, p. 147). First, Buber spoke of it as our personal wholeness before it split into its physical and psychic manifestations. Trüb felt the second way Buber used the unconscious was to define that which is split off from our wholeness when we say "no" to the dialogue (Friedman, 1985, p. 148). Trüb, Friedman, and Hycner (Hycner, 1991, pp. 156-157) have all spoken of the presence of our unconscious function when we say "no" to the meeting—when we abort the dialogue and do not respond with our unified wholeness. When we do not respond to the concrete event with our full potential, we are divided and fragmented. Parts of ourselves are cut off from the rest—becoming inaccessible and unconscious—defying our nature to be unified in our wholeness.

We may remove the discomfort of our fragmentation from our awareness, lock it away in forgetfulness, put its connections to other parts of ourselves out of awareness, rearrange its connections. The dialogical psychotherapist believes that when we define our psychological defenses from this perspective there is a clarity that would otherwise elude us. But these psychological defenses are ineffective, leaving us impotent in our struggle to unify our wholeness. We cannot set aside a part of our fragmented selves to do the unifying work without further fragmentation.

Case Example

The client's attempts to avoid the discomfort of his fragmentation by locking away certain connections or associations in forgetfulness is illustrated in Alex, an auto mechanic in his late twenties. He came to see me because of the discomfort he was experiencing in his relationship with his girlfriend. He reported that she had recently told him something about himself that he found very disturbing and he needed to talk about it. She had told him that he never felt like he was worthy of being loved. He always seemed to think that she did not love him, and she felt like she had to reassure him constantly. She had come to the conclusion that she could do nothing to make him feel she loved him. He would always want more proof and would never believe that she really cared for him.

In subsequent sessions, Alex revealed that his parents had always thought of him as a quitter. They constantly told him, as he was growing up, that he never finished anything he started. They continually reminded him of his inadequacies. He had learned to think of himself as inadequate and undeserving. I suggested that this feeling about himself might have something to do with his inability to believe his girlfriend really loved him. Although he stated that he could understand why I might make such a connection, I was wrong. There was no connection or he would not feel the way he did. He was certain that his girlfriend really did not love him in spite of her assurance. If she really loved him, he would feel it. The connection remained a mystery to him.

The mystery of this connection to Alex is understandable in view of his reported history of interactions with his parents. They never interacted with his wholeness. Their interactions with him did not include his possibility for feeling adequate and deserving of love. Consequently these feelings were severed from his unified wholeness—remaining unconscious. Until they were reclaimed he would not be able to utilize them, that is, to feel adequate and deserving in his relationship with his girlfriend. Yet, his psychological defense was designed to prevent this from happening. He had concluded that his inability to feel adequate and deserving of his girlfriend's love was not the problem. The problem, according to him, was that his girlfriend really did not love him in spite of her claiming otherwise.

Alex did not continue to see me. In my last contact with him he reported that he has been unable to find the kind of relationship he needs among his friends in order to gain access to his ability to feel good about himself. To imagine what was real for Alex was too uncomfortable for them. He reported that most of his friends tended to avoid him, and the few who did not, sought to capitalize on his bad feelings about himself. They extracted various favors from him in return for their continuing association with him. Alex continues to feel that his girlfriend does not love him. She finally left him and is now living with her family. He continues to feel that the way others treat him is because he is undeserving of any other kind of treatment. Alex has not been able to resolve his problem by analyzing it.

Unconscious as Aborted Psychic Activities

This is not to dismiss the importance of our I–It relations—our analytical abilities. Certainly, our cognitive function and the resulting accumulation of knowledge are vital to our survival. Our ability to analyze and synthesize our perceptions of our perceptions (apperception) produces an objective world that we can share with others. Our existence as embodied creatures makes our survival dependent on the creation of such a world, but the consequence of producing it cuts us off from our own uniqueness as well as that of the other, resulting in our fragmentation and inability to actualize the unique potential for being that resides in our wholeness.

Restoration of Wholeness Through Dialogue

We must reach beyond ourselves to the dialogue for unification and healing. Actualization of our wholeness can unfold only in our I–Thou relations. Therefore, both types of relations are necessary: our continued embodiment requires I–It relations; our personal wholeness requires I–Thou relations. The ontology of the between does not tell us how this occurs. It tells us only of the conditions necessary for its occurrence.

Case Example

The restoration of our wholeness in dialogue is illustrated in a client who came for treatment because of experiencing severe fragmentation. She complained of being extremely anxious and not being able to function comfortably in certain areas of her life. She was married, had several children, and among her other housekeeping chores did the laundry for the family. Although she liked washing clothes, lately she found herself becoming increasingly anxious each time she even thought of the task. By the time she entered the laundry she had become so distraught she could hardly remain in the room. Her distress would soon escalate to nausea, making it impossible for her to continue the task. This reaction had started three months prior to her coming to see me. It was causing serious problems for her husband who could not understand what was wrong with her.

As she sat before me, she pleaded for help. I thought, where do I start with a person with this kind of problem? She was describing anxiety attacks in her laundry room. I thought, as a good therapist, I should be able to summon all kinds of ideas for why this could be happening to my client, but they did not come. I felt stupid and inadequate. Then I felt anxious, confused, and irritated that I could not figure it out. Then I realized this must be the way she was feeling. I began to discuss with her how she felt about her dilemma. I could see that talking about it in an understanding and sympathetic manner seemed to comfort her. The topic of conversation moved away from her problem to other areas of her life. In the course of our conversation we often discussed her father. She felt he was distant and aloof from her. His coldness disturbed her very much. I began to notice that each time her father was discussed she became anxious. After several of these episodes, I suggested that she focus on her feelings when this occurred. She said she had been doing that and could not figure why it made her feel just like she did when she was doing the laundry.

As our meetings continued, I asked her to think of anything in the laundry room that reminded her of her father and the feelings she was having. I watched as a look of bewilderment came over her face. She seemed reluctant to share her thoughts with me, fearing I would think them foolish. I assured her that I thought we were dealing with the most important thing in her life in that moment and would not think anything she said about it was foolish. She responded, "Its the smell of the ripe olive tree in the back yard just outside the laundry room window that reminds me of my father. When I was a little girl, I seem to remember smelling it and getting sick. But why would that remind me of my father? He never came in the laundry room. My mother was always the one in there." At that point she became very anxious. I moved closer to her and attempted to stand with her in her encounter by sharing her thoughts and feelings. We were both feeling anxious and puzzled. She finally said she did not want to think of it any more. As she left the session, I thought it strange that neither of us could figure what was causing her anxiety. What does a ripe olive tree outside the laundry room window have to do with her father?

For several weeks I did not hear from her. I thought I had lost her. I had not been much help to her. But she did reappear. She said she had been out of town and had forgotten to call. I expressed my concern for her and told her how sorry I was that I had not been able to help her. For a moment our roles were reversed. She spent the next few minutes reassuring me. She told me how much my concern had meant to her. It was in this context that we were able to establish something between us that breached her fragmentation. Within a few moments she was exploring the connection between her smell of the ripe olive tree and her father. She was ready to stay with it until an answer came—and it came like a bombshell. She blurted out, "It was his sperm that smelled like the olive tree when he would come all over me in my bed at night." She stopped, startled by what she had just said. She then very calmly said, "Now where in the world did that come from? Why would I say something like that?" It was as if she had had nothing to do with the thought. Certainly it did not come from any suggestions or hints I might have given her.

Although the memory came from within her, her reclaiming of it was made possible by a reality that was beyond her. In our dialogue she had been able to reclaim that part of herself that had been severed by her father's sexual abuse, dividing and fragmenting her unified wholeness. The power to reclaim the severed part of herself was not found in either of us but in what our sharing had created between us, thus causing her to experience it as strange. It was the beginning of her healing journey.

Summation and Preview

To summarize, Buber felt that the nature of our personal wholeness is unconscious. Since it is beyond our conscious awareness, the unconscious can be said to be its guardian. Our personal wholeness is the base of our being, our essence. It is what we are intended to be. It is our potential for the expression of our uniqueness. It encompasses all our manifold possibilities to which we do not have conscious access. These possibilities remain nonconscious potentials until they are called out. When this occurs, they are split into their respective psychic (inner) and physical (outer) manifestations required for our conscious apprehension; they appear as dissociated phenomena since their source cannot be traced by introspection or analysis. Their manifestation is always precipitated by a concrete event. The event that calls them out seems to exist apart from ourselves and remains so in our interaction with it. It is distanced from and stands against us, calling for an interaction with it that will result in our potential being actualized. To respond to the concrete event with our whole potential is to follow our personal direction. When we do not respond to the event with our whole potential, we are left fragmented and divided. We are not conscious of our fragmented parts until we are restored to wholeness. Since our nature is to be unified, we experience this state of being as disturbing. Our attempts to restore our unity are seen in our psychological defenses and our dreams. However, the restoration can be found only in dialogue.

The dialogical therapist must be able to tolerate the mystery of our unconscious functions if the client is to experience the healing work of the between. When the client presents himself for treatment, he brings a wealth of possibilities for being that have never been realized. The therapist brings the possibility of interacting with the client in a dialogue that heals the client's fragmented and divided self and gives him access to his unique possibilities for being.

Although Friedman has not considered dreams as an element apart from the unconscious, because of their importance it seems appropriate to discuss them in a separate chapter (Hycner, 1991, pp. ix–x). Our dreams, unlike our unconscious, are not entirely pre-dialogical. The dialogical psychotherapist contends that our dreams are the product of incomplete dialogues, and it is possible for us to relate to them as existing apart from ourselves for the sake of dialogue. Our dreams can be viewed as unfinished dialogues that need to be completed. Our dreams have something to say to us if we are willing to engage them in dialogue.

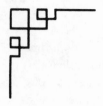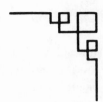

8

Dreams

Buber held that dreams, like personal wholeness, can never be known directly. He even questioned whether we know or have dreams at all. He contended that all we possess is the memory of our relation to the dream, but nothing of the dream itself (Friedman, 1985, p. 155). Yet, we have all experienced times when there is a transitional state between sleeping and awaking, not unlike the sensation of floating up from the dream as we are aroused from our sleeping state. In this state, we experience something we will probably lose if we do not do something with it, for we have not yet remembered or thought about it. The moment we reflect on it, our conscious mind shapes and elaborates it, and we are aware of struggling to mold this something in a fashion that can be tolerated by consciousness.

The Elusiveness of Dreams

Often we are aware of leaving something behind when communicating the dream, something that lies beyond the pale of our shaping. Our spoken language cannot communicate it effectively. It is a private something that cannot be shared in its entirety with others. Sometimes it seems so bizarre or frightening that we make no effort to continue shaping it and whatever has been shaped is quickly willed from our awareness. In all these instances, our memory is wrestling with something; yet, as Buber contended, we cannot be in direct contact with it. This something is our dream.

We cannot know with certainty the origin of dreams. They may simply be sensations elicited by the random firing of the neurons in the brain that are peculiar to sleep. They may come directly from the unconscious. They may be residual sensations of our conscious that have not been or cannot be processed and assimilated appropriately. However, if we relate to our dreams in an analytical or dialectical fashion (I–It), they present us with an illogic and contradiction that are not available to our conscious world. We see this in the ways sensations from our recent and past conscious experiences are presented without respect for order, connections, or time and space.

Friedman has said: "We cannot speak of dream relations as if they were identical with relations to persons in waking life. What we can say is that having set the dream over against us, thus isolated, shaped, elaborated, and given form as an independent opposite, we enter into dialogue with it. From now on it becomes one of the realities that addresses us in the world, just as surely and as concretely as any so-called external happening" (1985, p. 197).

The Dream as Door to Dialogue

Our dreams present the opportunity for dialogue, if we are willing to attribute them to meetings that have been aborted or to unfulfilled dialogues that have occurred in our waking moments. To the extent that there is dialogue with our dreams, there is an opportunity to experience and complete the unfulfilled work of the meeting. It is not unusual for us to have similar dreams over and over until the unifying work of the dialogue is completed.

The meaning of the dream is always tied to the client's unique struggle for wholeness. This has significant implications for dialogical psychotherapy. The dialogical psychotherapist does not attempt to interpret the client's dreams by imposing her own preconceived notions or theory, nor is it possible for the client to utilize his shaping memory to analyze the meaning of his dream (I-It). The dream occurs when he fails to respond with his whole potential to the meeting; it presents an opportunity for him to restore his fragmented self by continuing the interaction to its completion. Thus, the task of the therapist is to assist the client to complete the dialogue (I-Thou) without imposing her interpretation on the dream (I-It).

It is possible for the therapist to analyze the dream (I-It) by focusing on its content and determining what each particular aspect of the dream symbolizes or what process is unfolding. However, in the analysis, as in all I-It relations, the therapist experiences only the abstractions that are commonly agreed on by the convention of meanings supplied by her theoretical orientation and nothing significant changes in the client as a result of the therapist's experience. If the client tries to analyze his own dreams, he will have the same result.

Dialogue with the Dream

We do not attain our wholeness as a result of our experience of ourselves, but in our relationship with the other, which changes both us and the other. One cannot have a dialogue with him- or herself; a dialogue requires the participation of the whole self, and it is impossible for one part of a self to interact with another part of the self while remaining whole. In the case of unfulfilled dialogues, however, our dreams have the peculiar ability to function as the other partner of the relationship, making dialogue possible between the dreamer and the remembered dream. Hycner calls this a *self-dialogue;* it is not really dialogue but dialectic since it takes place within us and not between us and another (Hycner, 1991, p. 51). This interaction, which only the client can have since he alone possesses the dream, completes the aborted dialogue that prompted the dream and creates a new reality (the between) that changes him. The therapist's role in such cases cannot be minimized, for it is his dialogue with the client that facilitates the client's dialogue with his dreams.

Something similar to the futility of dream analysis may be seen in our struggle to make sense of our conscious shaping and elaboration of certain psychological traumata, drug states, or psychosis. However, in these cases the shaping is not confined to our dreams but deals with a much more extended area of our conscious life. There is an absence of dialogue between us and the manifestations of others, resulting in a fragmentation that is intolerable to self-unity. The shaping memory attempts to deal with this fragmentation as it does in dream analysis, but meaning in the situation cannot be found in I-It relations. The only solution is to reestablish the dialogue (I-Thou). In some instances, the possibility of the dialogue occurring is enhanced by rather straightforward remedies, such as abstinence from drugs, restoration of our physical condition after injury, or removal from the situation that produced the trauma. Sometimes psychotherapy is needed for healing to occur. Healing must come from a resource outside the disturbed self in the dialogue between the client and therapist.

Case Examples

An example of a client who used dreams for healing is Jean. She was single and her presenting problem was her impending breakup with her lover who was in his fifties. She complained that she had always had older men as lovers, but the relationships never seemed to work out. Her present lover, like all the others, seemed to want her only for sex and not companionship. Although she liked pleasing men sexually, she always wanted more from the relationship. Yet, she had difficulty explaining exactly what she wanted. She could only find excitement with older men.

After several sessions, Jean began to speak of her dreams. She found them quite perplexing and insisted that I interpret them for her. I told her the dreams spoke to her, not to me, and only she could relate to them .She complained that she did not understand how she could relate to a dream. I asked her to consider what the dreams were saying to her and what she wished to say to her dreams. She began by including me in her considerations as she struggled to interact with her dreams. It seemed that the more she struggled, the more often new dreams appeared with slight variations. It became increasingly apparent to her that the dreams had to do with where she played when she was a little girl. In all the dreams, there was a large house with many rooms. First, she played in an upstairs room by herself with someone else playing in another part of the same room. The safety of the other person worried her. In a subsequent dream, she was playing in a room downstairs with a younger man. In a later dream, the young man was playing in another room separate from her but still downstairs. The dream told her how happy she was that the young man had finally found a safe place in the house to play. She was perplexed about this and wondered why it was so. Was it because he was in a room separate from hers? She asked herself, was she a menace to him?

As Jean continued her struggle to relate to her dreams, the answers to her inquiries began to come. She began to recall that when she was a little girl, her father would come into her bedroom at night, the same room where her younger brother was sleeping, and molest her. She began to feel again a forgotten concern for her younger brother. She was concerned that he might awaken and see what the father was doing to her. She spoke of her fear that the father might also harm him.

After this, she began to understand why she felt that the young man in her dream was safe when he slept in another bedroom. She had never spoken to her younger brother about the father's abuse. After some consideration, she decided it was a dialogue that needed to take place. She called her brother, who was living in another part of the country, and shared her childhood concerns for him. She reported that he was deeply moved and felt that what she had told him helped him to understand his own uncomfortable and distant relationship with the father. She reported in subsequent sessions that both she and her brother experienced healing in their lives as a result of her dialogues with her dreams and her subsequent dialogue with him. The last time I saw her, she had not yet decided to share her dialogue with her father.

Another client, Jim, also found healing in dialogues with his dreams. Jim was single, irascible, and approaching fifty. He had recently suffered a stroke, resulting in his forced retirement. He had been referred because of his hostile reactions to the frustrations of an inactive life, which caused his blood pressure to rise to a level endangering his health. The presenting problem was to teach Jim how to live with his day-to-day frustrations now that he no longer had a job.

Jim struggled to find a way to share his dilemma with me. For some time, he did not feel I could understand what he was going through. I struggled also to imagine what Jim was feeling. It was some time before there was sufficient inclusion on my part for Jim to trust me. It was after this that Jim began to tell me of his dreams. The content of his dreams varied except for the constant recurrence of his boots. In his dreams, sometimes he had lost one of his boots and could not find it. On other occasions, he could not get his boots on because they did not fit. In one of his sessions, he turned to me and said, "What's with this damn boot thing? It's driving me crazy. You're the shrink. You tell me what it means." I replied that I did not know, but I was willing to share his quest to find what it meant. For several sessions, off and on, Jim and I would ponder what the boots were trying to tell him. He would come into the session and say, "Those damned boots showed up in my dreams again last night."

After several weeks, Jim came into the session very excited. He had finally figured what the boots in his dreams were trying to tell him. They were cowboy boots. President Reagan wore cowboy boots. The president was still going strong and he was going to fight his forced retirement and did not intend to stop working until President Reagan did. Although Jim was not able to regain his job, he began showing remarkable adjustment to the frustrations in his life—such as having to stand in line for something, or being forced to wait when a car in front of him lingered too long at a stop sign. Just being around people had previously made Jim angry, but now he began to report different feelings. Maybe people were not really as bad as he had thought. He began to respond to the relaxation techniques I had taught him to lower his blood pressure. He started keeping extensive records of his successes. He reported that he had been able to drop his blood pressure so low that his doctor was alarmed. Jim took great delight in showing his doctor how he could raise and lower his pressure by relaxation techniques. His attitude had changed from one of cynicism and bitterness to delight in his ability to cope with situations that had previously frustrated him.

As Jim had said, "I just had to learn to find those damned boots and wear them every day, just like President Reagan."

Another illustration of a healing dialogue with our dreams was an adolescent client who believed his father did not understand him. Each time he attempted to discuss his school curriculum with his father, his father always brought up his own childhood athletic history. The father had insisted, according to the adolescent, that his son play baseball; the boy did, but injured his knees, requiring an operation. He could not communicate with his father and felt he never listened to his wishes, insisting that the boy follow in the father's footsteps and be involved in the school's athletic program.

In this context, the adolescent's ongoing attempts to communicate with his father, he presented his dream. In his latest dream he was attacked by a humanlike thing that continually changed shapes and had appeared under varying conditions in his previous dreams. He was aware in his dream that if he waited, it would eventually change into a shape he could handle. Eventually it changed into a little boy. At this point, he grabbed the child and beat it against the wall, hoping to kill it. But the little character simply would not die, no matter how hard he slammed it against the wall. Finally, it was subdued, but the dream ended before the dreamer could know whether the boy was dead.

When he was asked to seek what the dream was trying to tell him, he was bewildered and could not think of anything. The dream was so rich with meaning for me, the therapist, I could hardly constrain myself from interpreting it for him. However, the dream was attempting to speak to the client and not the therapist. After pondering for some time, he was horrified at what he had done. In the midst of his revulsion, he suddenly burst out laughing. He then said with great joy, "I just killed that little sucker. That something that changed shape was my dad. It was his little boy. The one that always harps on me to play sports. That's the one I tried to kill." He continued to be amused at what he had done for several minutes before he thought of how this might affect his relationship with his father. The dream addressed the unfinished business, the aborted dialogue, that existed between them. The ramifications of his dialogue with the dream were played out in subsequent dialogue with his father.

Summation and Preview

Of course, in all three of these cases, much more was going on with the client than was discussed in the presentation. At the risk of appearing to oversimplify the therapeutic process, I have restricted my comments to illustrate client use of dreams in a therapeutic dialogue. It is possible that the dreams possessed much more potential for dialogue than was utilized by the clients in the illustrations. However, from the dialogical perspective, it is the client's dream and it speaks to him, regardless of its rich potential for interpretation from the therapist's theoretical point of view.

The therapist has a supporting role when the client is discovering the message of his dreams, but in a client-therapist dialogue, the therapist must be totally involved with all aspects of the client's experience. *Inclusion* is the term used to define the therapist's ability to experience the client's reality as being as real as her own, and at the same time retain an awareness of her own existence as separate and apart from him. It is her ability to move beyond empathy and identification to the actual experience of the client's existence that makes the dialogue possible. An understanding of it is necessary to the practice of dialogical psychotherapy. Inclusion is discussed in the next chapter.

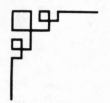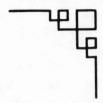

9

Inclusion

Inclusion has been referred to as "imagining the real." It is a way of imagining the other in his unique wholeness in the most real way possible. This act involves conceiving what the other, the desired partner of the dialogue, is thinking, wishing, feeling, and perceiving. Buber has spoken of it as "a bold swinging, demanding the most intensive stirring of one's being into the life of the other" (Buber, 1988, p. 71). Inclusion means seeing the definite otherness of the partner and his uniqueness. It means seeing the other concretely without reduction or abstraction.

Distinction from Identification and Empathy

The initiator of inclusion, the therapist, has a presence that is in immediate and direct contact with the other, yet still in contact with her own self. In this respect, inclusion is different from identifica-

This chapter is based primarily on private conversations with Maurice Friedman and on selections from his book, *The Healing Dialogue in Psychotherapy* (1985), Chapter 17.

tion or empathy. To the extent that she *identifies* with the other, she sees only herself in the other; she relates only to those parts of the other that are similar to herself. This type of relating does irreparable damage to the other's unique wholeness. The other is no longer related to as a Thou, but as an It. To the extent that she *empathizes* with the other, she experiences only the other's self and loses contact with herself, thus precluding the possibility of relating. The I is lost in the other.

Making Contact

The act of inclusion allows one to make contact with another and still be in contact with one's own self. If the other responds to our reaching out (our act of inclusion), contact is made. This contact is not just from one to the other but exists between them. This unique reality of the between is present in all genuine dialogue.

Inclusion is necessary but not sufficient for the dialogue to occur. Inclusion is initiated by the therapist but the client must respond. Yet, the therapist initiates inclusion at some risk to herself. She must be willing to give up the relative comfort of her own being by boldly swinging over and encompassing the sick being of the other. She will be changed by the experience in ways that she cannot predict if she is to allow all of the client's impulses to affect her, and she cannot be certain of the outcome. She must, in those moments that she practices inclusion, give up control of the outcome to the reality of the between.

The dialogical psychotherapist practices inclusion in those moments when she views the fragmentation and the resulting conflicts within the client. In such cases, the therapist must be able to glimpse the whole unique person within the fragmented one as a prerequisite to the dialogue. She must see the absence of unity, generating chaos and despair in the client. When both the therapist and the client agree that this fragmented state is not the optimal condition for the client and both are mutually open to the intimacy involved in sharing the client's problems, there is the possibility of initiating healing.

The therapist is not gifted with omniscience; she cannot know how the client's fragmentation is to be fixed. She need only know that among the manifold possibilities that exist between herself and the client, there is a way to restore the client's wholeness. From the interaction of the therapist and the client, the client is able to apprehend and actualize the possibility of wholeness that exists between them. The healing comes from this meeting. Inclusion is necessary for genuine dialogue. Without a clear understanding of it, the therapist will only frustrate the healing work of the between.

Growth from Interhuman Contacts

Buber contends that our subjective growth does not come from our intrapersonal efforts. It comes from interhuman concerns between us and the other. It comes from that which is between individuals, not that which is within an individual (Buber, 1988, p. 61). In such instances we are also made present, in the sense that we are caused to appear—to exist—in our greatest potential. This is a mutual experience as the other partner in the dialogue has a similar experience.

How does this happen? It is like seeing oneself on the television monitor or in a mirror. The video camera and the mirror let us view our body's shape, our movements, and other aspects of our demeanor that ordinarily we can't see. The presence of one partner in his wholeness is like a mirror that totally encompasses the other, letting him see his whole self. The presence of the wholeness of one provides the same mirroring for the other.

Seeing the Whole Person

Making the other present requires mutual acceptance, affirmation, and confirmation. It demands an acceptance that embraces the other's wholeness without judgment or protestation. When these mutual conditions prevail, each of the partners is made present to the other.

To experience the other in his wholeness, however, without reduction or abstraction, is extremely difficult for most therapists. By training, we are accustomed first to taking the client apart in order to understand him and then to relate to him in the light of our analysis. However, the client, in his struggle to gain acceptance, has learned to present himself to the world in two different manners, which Buber has called "being and seeming" (Buber, 1988, pp. 65–68). When he is in the throes of seeming, he is more concerned about how others see him than in being true to what he really is. He goes about attempting to manipulate the reaction of others by appearing in a way that is calculated to gain their acceptance. When the client is in this state, it is difficult for the therapist to relate to him as he truly is intended to be. It is at this point that our psychology fails us, for the client in this state does not know himself who he is. His deception has cut him off from his real being. Our psychology may tell us how he has accomplished his deception, but it will not tell us what he is intended to be. The answer lies in his unified wholeness.

How do we access his wholeness? We must remove ourselves from a reliance on the analytical method of our human sciences and seek to imagine what is real for the client. It is a most powerful commitment of the therapist to experience in her imagination what the client is thinking, feeling, and perceiving at that moment. It is a bold move that demands the most intensive stirring of our being into the life of the client (Buber, 1988, p. 71).

Case Examples

To exercise the gift of inclusion takes courage on the part of the therapist. She must be willing to go places with the client that are unexpected and not always comfortable. Without a commitment to endure such states, she will fail, as I did with Harry. This client was in his early thirties, married, with no children. He was evasive and uneasy in the initial session. Toward the end of the session he spoke briefly about his problem, saying that it was unusual and that he was not comfortable talking about it. I searched within myself to find some way to gain his confidence. Nothing came to me. Since the session was almost over, I suggested that we deal with his problem in the next session. I explained that the first session was often spent in getting acquainted and learning to be comfortable with each other. He left without discussing the nature of his problem.

I felt bad about my inability to make contact with Harry and determined in the next session to gain his trust and acceptance. I decided the best course of action was just to accept the situation and embrace his distrust as his way of relating to me. As I relaxed into my acceptance, he began to feel more comfortable and started talking about the nature of his problem. He described his relationship with his father who had been living with him since his mother had died. At first he was happy to have his father with him, but lately the father had become more and more dependent on him, demanding most of his time, to the dismay of his wife. His wife wanted to have children but felt it was impossible with his father in the home. Harry said he was caught in a hopeless bind. He wanted to move his father into a convalescent home but could not bring himself to do it, even at the insistence of his wife. He vacillated between anger and guilt.

As Harry sat before me I began to imagine what it must be like for him. In the ensuing moments I was caught up in his dilemma. I could feel his guilt over wanting to care for his father at the same time he wanted to send him away. Yet, I could also sense his desperate desire to support his wife and start a family of his own. In those moments, as he sat before me weeping, I found the pain of his frustration unbearable. I could not hold back my own tears. It was more than I could stand. The feelings I was having were totally unexpected. I was not prepared for the devastating effect that sharing Harry's reality would have upon me. I am sorry to say that at the end of the session I withdrew from the situation. I told him that there was no way I could be of help to him. He had a practical problem and not a psychological one. Because of my unwillingness to share his pain, I failed him as a therapist and myself as the person I was intended to be. I can only hope that he was able to obtain the help of someone else who would remain with him in his pain until he was able to resolve his problem and healing could take place.

If he allows it, the therapist can use such an experience as a means of growth. A short time after my experience with Harry, another client offered me such an opportunity. Jenny was in her forties. She had been married and had three children. Jenny was a transsexual and was undergoing a sex change. The time had arrived for her to tell her children of her impending surgery. Jenny's ex-wife had known of her transsexualism for some time but the children had not been told. Jenny had left her wife and children in another state before beginning her transition from male to female.

She asked me to meet with her former wife and children to tell them of her gender change.

As Jenny's family entered my office, I began to feel the anguish of both Jenny and her ex-wife. The mother had told me on the phone how much the children loved their father and how much they had missed him. As the children seated themselves across the room from their father in preparation for the meeting, I could feel their happiness at being with their father for the first time in several months. They waited with happy anticipation for the meeting to begin. Their mother had told them that their daddy had some important news to share with them. I watched as Jenny stumbled for the words to tell the children that their daddy was soon to disappear from their lives. She had dressed as a male for the meeting.

As Jenny explained her impending sex change, I watched first the surprise, then the look of bewilderment that came over the faces of the children. The teenage daughter began to sob and the two younger children, seven and ten years of age, soon followed. The mother then addressed them in a very loving manner. She spoke of her love for their father and how that love had compelled her to support him in his need to become a woman even though it meant she would lose him as her husband. She went on to explain to the children how miserable their father had been as a male and how happy he now was as a female. She spoke to them of the way love expresses itself. Love wants what is best for the person; if they loved their father, they must find a way within themselves to accept his sex change. At this point we were all in tears.

I suggested we find some way for the children to express their feelings about what had been asked of them. It was a heart-wrenching event. The ten-year-old son haltingly asked his father, "How can I help you, Daddy?" Jenny, responding through her tears, asked that if his son could, would he accept the fact that his father was dead? The youngster struggled with his answer but said he would try. In the ensuing conversation it was decided that they must each say good-bye to their father, understanding that after the meeting he, as their father, would disappear from their lives. When they met him again, he would be like an aunt. He would still love them but would not be their father any more. He stated that he realized it was hard for them, but he could do nothing about it if he was to be who he truly was. In that moment, I felt the pain and confusion in the children. The silence became almost unbearable. My strongest desire was to close the meeting and escape the pain, but there was still work to be done. This time I was determined to stay the course, no matter how difficult. As the children said good-bye to their father, I cannot express the depth of my anguish. I watched as the smaller children arose from their seats, walked over to their father, embraced him, and told him how much they loved him and how sorry they were to lose him. There was a dignity in their actions that was not pretense but came from deep within each child.

In that meeting I stood with the family in their suffering. Needless to say, I was taken to places where I have never been before. The meeting brought significant changes in me. I had been strength-ened in a way that allowed me to accept my client's pain and imbued with the knowledge that healing can occur even in the most hopeless situations if you stand with the client. I had stayed with the family. What occurred between the children and me has become a part of my ongoing existence. I shall never be the same as a result of the meeting. I have since heard from the mother and the children. They sent me a Christmas card thanking me for helping their father to become who he was truly intended to be.

Summation and Preview

Inclusion is the means by which the therapist enters the world of the client by being present with him. At times it is accomplished at great cost to the therapist. It requires that she go without defenses into a reality often fraught with fear, anxiety, and psychic pain. I must add that there are also times when the therapist, in her inclu-sion, is privileged to share the joy and excitement of the client's triumphs—to experience the wonder of the client's growth. Inclu-sion defines the way she stands with the client in the most real manner possible in her desire for his healing. There are no thera-peutic skills or techniques that can be substituted for inclusion. For some therapists it may be too great a price to pay, but for the dia-logical psychotherapist it is the only path to the client's healing.

Because the client comes to the dialogue for help and the

therapist comes to give help, the interaction of each is affected by their respective intentions. This presents a problem with mutuality in the therapeutic encounter. In the next chapter I will discuss how this problem affects the dialogue, what the responsibilities of the therapist are, and how they are addressed in the mutuality of the therapeutic dialogue.

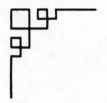
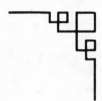

10

Mutuality

Mutuality in the therapeutic dialogue is different from that of friend with friend. In both cases, as Friedman has pointed out, there is mutual contact: both partners experience the presence of the other in an open and direct manner, and there is mutual trust in that both partners in either case are open and present to each other. There is mutual concern as the partners share the problems presented in the dialogue. However, in a therapeutic dialogue, there is no mutual inclusion, as in a friendship. In a therapeutic dialogue, inclusion comes from the therapist's side of the relationship but not necessarily from the client's side. The therapist does not expect the client to imagine what the therapist is thinking, feeling, and willing in the therapeutic relationship. The focus is on the client and not the therapist.

The feelings that emerge from the therapeutic dialogue are assumed to be intrinsic to that particular relationship. They are not

This section is based primarily on private conversations with Maurice Friedman and on selections from his book, *The Healing Dialogue in Psychotherapy* (1985), Chapter 16.

familiar feelings that have been acquired in previous relationships and brought to the therapeutic dialogue, such as in cases of transference. They are uniquely derived from the current relationship, which has resulted from the therapist's inclusion.

Dangers of Presumptuousness and Enmeshment

Inclusion in the therapeutic dialogue presents a twofold danger to the therapist, presumptuousness and enmeshment. The therapist must at all times be aware of his special relationship with the client and, even in the most intimate moments of sharing, must suppress his own needs and concerns and look to those of the patient. He must take care not to presume to shape the client's personal direction but leave the outcome to the work of the between that evolves from the relationship between them. In those moments when he practices inclusion, the therapist is exposed and vulnerable to the psychic pain of the client and must remain present to his own self lest he become enmeshed in the client's problems. If healing is to occur, the client must also understand that he is a partner in the relationship and must not expect the therapist to resolve his problem. The client must take responsibility for pursuing the unique direction he discovers in the relationship.

Exploitation and Lack of Inclusion

Inclusion is an ongoing problem in the therapeutic encounter. It must be revisited time and again if the relationship is to retain its therapeutic nature. As humans, we are particularly dependent on the help of others. As infants, we rely on our caretakers for a longer period of time than any other species. We are usually in our second decade of development before we are considered able to survive on our own. Other anthropoids accomplish this task well within their first decade of existence. It is assumed that our caretakers know what is best for us, and it is their responsibility to care for us during this prolonged period of dependency. Our extended dependency makes us especially vulnerable to exploitation by our caretakers. Most of the abuse we experience stems from relationships in which we were dependent on others for our care. In a relationship in which the other partner ostensibly is trustworthy and concerned in his contact with us but does not understand the personal nature of our problem, inclusion is absent.

Such exploitation often extends into adulthood. The helper assumes that he knows what the other was intended to be in the situation. This knowing does not come from his inclusion. When one projects his own needs and wants on another, the other usually experiences the helper as judgmental and condescending and feels inept and guilty because he has not responded in the appropriate manner. As a result of the relationship, he feels something is wrong with him.

Often in marital counseling the husband or wife will relate to the other partner without inclusion. In such cases, the husband may say, "Doctor, yesterday I came home after a hard day and started to tell my wife what happened to me at work." At this point, it is evident that he had been hurt and needed her to understand and be concerned for him. He knows that although she does not have the power to fix his feelings, she does have the ability to be present with him as he deals with his hurt.

The husband continues his narration of the interaction, "She attacked me. All I did was tell her what happened and she began telling me what I had done wrong. God, all I wanted was for her to understand how it hurt me to be treated that way and dammed if she didn't start treating me the same way they had treated me at work. What's wrong with her? The last thing I needed was for her to jump at me like that." In that moment of asking for help, he placed himself in a very vulnerable position. He was dependent on her. She had the ability to help or hurt him. He was not seeking advice or condemnation from his wife but her inclusion. The response in such interactions determines the nature of their relationship.

If the wife is asked to give her account of the interaction, she usually replies with something like, "Well, what does he expect me to do? I get so upset when he tells me how they have treated him on the job that I can hardly stand it. He ought to stop letting them treat him that way." If we are inclusive with her, we can experience her hurt in the interaction. She was disturbed and threatened by what had happened to her husband. She cares for him but feels impotent to protect him from the hurt. Out of her frustration at being asked to do something she did not know how to do, she attacked him with advice that he felt was condescending. Her mistake was in trying to solve the problem for him instead of standing with him and allowing that which arose between them to comfort his hurt.

I have found such encounters to be common in couples who come for help. There is an absence of inclusion. The hurt that comes from these encounters generates animosity and misunderstanding and prevents the pair from developing an understanding of each other. Each always understands the other only from his or her own point of view instead of making the other present by inclusion. Neither attempts to stand in the place of the other. Yet, each will adamantly proclaim understanding the other only too well. "I know all his tricks to get my sympathy." "She thinks she understands me, Doctor, but she doesn't have any idea about how I feel." It is little wonder that they usually feel they have a communication problem.

The same problems occur in parent-child relationships. The parent and the child are unable to communicate with each other. Some of the most dramatic breakthroughs I have had with both children and adolescents have been when I stood with them and experienced the way they saw the world. The child feels that at last someone understands. Most of his life, he has experienced himself in helping relationships that are devoid of inclusion. He has been constantly asked why he did something, but the questioner would not listen to his reply with understanding and concern. Successful therapy with a youngster who has such a history of disregard must focus on building a trusting relationship with him. This comes only when the youngster has consistently experienced the therapist's regard for his feelings and concerns, as shown in the case of Adele.

Case Example

She was an eight-year-old female client whose adoptive mother was concerned because she was failing in school. Adele had been adopted the year before seeing me. The current school year was the first year she had attended school since the death of her biological mother. She had always done well in school but was now failing. The teacher reported to the mother that Adele was not paying attention in the classroom. She daydreamed throughout most of the school day, did not listen to the teacher, and never finished her classroom assignments.

I spent several sessions with Adele talking and playing with her before she trusted me enough to share her innermost thoughts. She explained that she could not tell her mother what was happening because she would think she did not love her, and if she told her teacher, the teacher might tell her mother. I told her that she could tell me, and I promised her that her mother would not be hurt. It was then that she shared her dark secrets with me. I was deeply touched as this small, eight-year-old youngster bared her soul to me. Throughout her sharing I was keenly aware of the trust she was placing in me and was humbled by her dependence on me to understand as she spoke of how much she missed her dead mother. She stated that all she thought of in school was how it used to be when she was with her mother and how much she loved her. She spoke of her need to know where her mother was now and if she was happy. With such heavy thoughts on her mind, it had been impossible for her to concentrate on her school work.

Shortly thereafter, with the benefit of modeling clay, we built a coffin, placed her mother in it, and said good-bye to her. We then placed her in a safe place in my office where she would be happy. Adele seemed relieved; shortly thereafter her teacher reported that she was doing much better.

But Adele had more secrets to share with me. It seems she had been taking things from others and hiding them in her bedroom as well as her playhouse in the backyard of her home. Her way of sharing with me was to use the modeling clay to recreate the objects she had taken. Before we had finished, my office floor was covered with things she had stolen from school, neighbors, and family. Afterward, she gave a sigh of relief and told me how good it felt to tell someone. I obtained a pledge from her mother that there would be no repercussion for Adele if I told her of the things that Adele had stolen. Her new mother was both amazed and relieved. Adele's confession explained the mysterious disappearance of objects that had been puzzling the family and neighbors for months. Later, Adele retrieved most of the missing objects and returned them to their owners with apologies. Her new mother reported she was doing well in school and they had developed a much closer relationship. I said good-bye to Adele and thanked her for trusting me to understand her.

Necessity for Trust

In order for me to help Adele it was necessary for her to trust me. As her therapist, I was not called on to make the same kind of commitment to her. The focus was on her concerns and I was not asked to tell her my secrets. The therapeutic relationship is not mutual and leaves the client vulnerable to exploitation by the therapist. There is always the danger that the therapist will attempt to impose his own expectations and demands on the client instead of fostering the client's uniqueness in the situation. This is a difficult issue that arises from the *problem of mutuality* in the therapeutic encounter. At what point does the therapist respond and when does he remain silent and allow the client to find his own way? How does the therapist respond to the client's request, "Doctor, please tell me what I should do"?

The dialogical psychotherapist contends that because of the nature of the dialogue, the therapist may be called on to speak to the client in a more direct manner than is acceptable in other therapeutic approaches. The inclusion of the therapist has produced an involvement with the client of an extremely intimate nature, which has generated a new reality between them. It is a reality that impacts both the client and the therapist. Out of this reality the therapist may be called on to speak to the client. But the client is not asked to speak to the personal concerns of the therapist.

Double Responsibility of Therapist

There is a danger of exploiting the client when the therapist tries to speak outside of dialogue. When the therapist does his work outside dialogue, he no longer encounters the unique wholeness of the client. The client is encountered as a set of symptoms that need to be ameliorated so he can function appropriately in the world. To function appropriately means to comply with the standards of conduct that are acceptable to our society. What is dealt with are those things that cause discomfort in the client or society in the light of these standards. There is little or no concern for the client's uniqueness or his personal direction. It is a safe and comfortable way for the therapist to conduct himself in the therapeutic endeavor.

On the other hand, if the therapist remains silent in the dialogue and does not speak out, he betrays the trust of the client. His intimate contact with the client in the dialogue brings into existence a concern that must be honored. By not speaking out he does not share with the client what the dialogue has uniquely imparted to him. Not to speak out is to betray the person he has become as a result of the dialogue. In this respect the therapeutic dialogue is not mutual. It is the client who comes to the meeting seeking help and in the process becomes vulnerable to exploitation by the therapist. Because the client risks more, the therapist's responsibility with regard to their mutual contact, trust, and concern is greater.

The therapeutic dialogue provides a setting in which the client can experience his unique wholeness—a setting that not only embraces the client's wholeness but also mirrors the wholeness of the therapist. Because of the realness of the therapist's exposure in the therapeutic dialogue, we should not minimize its impact on him. The fact that the therapeutic dialogue always challenges the therapist to pursue the client's concern does not mean that the therapist is called on to neglect his own needs in the encounter. To the contrary, out of the therapeutic dialogue comes a reality that transcends the concerns of both therapist and client—a reality in which the concerns of the therapist address the concerns of the client and the concerns of the client address the concerns of the therapist.

Summation and Preview

The problems associated with mutuality in the therapeutic encounter can be resolved only in dialogue. The dialogical psychotherapist holds that outside of dialogue the lack of mutuality in the therapeu-

tic encounter can be threatening. The relationship can quickly dete-
riorate into an interaction in which both may assume that the therapist has a better grasp of the client's problems than the client
himself. Control and manipulation of the client become an issue.
The therapist may assume he knows what is best for the client
without considering the fulfillment of the client's uniqueness. He
does not receive his impetus from the reality of the between but from
within his self; this may be manifested in an arrogant fashion that
is detrimental to the client. Taking control also places an unreal-
istic burden on the therapist as he attempts to manipulate the outcome of his encounter with the client. To heal the fragmented self
of the client outside of dialogue is an impossible task for the therapist. In order to be effective the therapist must always be mindful
and respectful of the ontology of the mysterious healing between.

The therapist's response to the therapeutic dialogue is manifested in his confirmation of the client. Confirmation requires him
to encourage the client to pursue his personal direction. He must
confirm the client in what the client is intended to be. Apart from
the dialogue he has no mandate; his concerns for the client may be
no more than the projection of his own wishes and desires on the
client and not the pursuit of the client's personal direction. True
confirmation is always found in the therapeutic dialogue—in what
the interaction says to the therapist about the client. Confirmation
will be discussed in the following chapter.

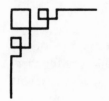
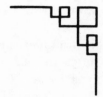

11

Confirmation

Although inclusion is necessary for confirmation, confirmation is more than inclusion. Confirmation involves the therapist's struggle with the client to discover and pursue the demands of the client's uniqueness. One of the basic presuppositions of dialogical psychotherapy is that each of our lives has a unique personal direction. This direction is the fulfillment of our uniqueness, and only as we pursue our personal direction with our totality can we find meaning and purpose in our lives. Since each of us holds manifold possibilities of being, we can have an existence without regard for our personal direction. In such cases, the absence of direction in our lives, for whatever reasons, produces chaos and despair, often resulting in mental and emotional disorders that require psychotherapy.

Our personal direction cannot be preconceived or preordained. It unfolds in our encounters with others. What we become is determined by our response to what is called out by each of these

This section is based primarily on private conversations with Maurice Friedman and on selections from his book, *The Healing Dialogue in Psychotherapy* (1985), Chapters 10, 11, and 12.

encounters. It is not found within ourselves but comes into being between us and what is not ourselves. We set out on the path of our personal direction when we are open to and accept the uniqueness encountered in each person and respond with wholeness.

For most of us, the fear of uncertainty in our lives interferes with our finding our direction. We seek to orient ourselves by looking for the differences and similarities in each event so that we may have the comfort of responding in a general way. Although such orienting is necessary to our ongoing existence in the world, it interferes with our ability to relate to others in a more human way. The pursuit of our personal direction is thwarted to the extent that we do not respond to the uniqueness of the event in an I-Thou relationship. Only in our encounters with the uniqueness of others, through dialogue, do we find our personal direction.

The Meaning of Confirmation

The goal of dialogical psychotherapy is to assist the client in the discovery and pursuit of his personal direction. This may involve exploring with him the barriers that have obstructed this pursuit, such as seeming to be something he is not in order to obtain the approval of others. The therapist and the client must look together at the constraints placed on the client in his childhood, parental and societal expectations, and other barriers. In this context, the therapist confirms the client. She knows the client in all that he has been, is now, and can be. This does not mean that the therapist accepts all that the client is now, but she acknowledges his current existence as a fact. Confirmation is the way the therapist, through the therapeutic dialogue, struggles with the client to meet the demands associated with the discovery and pursuit of his unique personal direction. Confirmation unfolds in the dialogue as the therapist confirms the uniqueness of the client in the pursuit of his personal direction. Confirmation by others is an ontological given that is essential to our existence as human beings (Buber, 1988, p. 61).

I have observed clients being able to respond to the problem that precipitated the dialogue in a unique way that has effected positive, significant changes in their lives. On one occasion after a client and I had experienced an encounter in the between, he left

the session shaken. On returning for the next session, he opened by
saying, "I don't know what happened the last time we met, but
something changed in me. I have felt much better. It was like I
really felt something with you that I always wanted to have with
my father. It has changed me. I'm just different somehow." In a
subsequent session I had with his wife, she also remarked on how
her husband had changed. "Jeffrey is different since he has been
seeing you. I don't know what happened, but he is different now
and for the better."

In my interaction with Jeffrey, I not only accepted him as he
was in that moment but also struggled with him, in the context of
the dialogue, for him to be more. We call this struggle with the
client *confirmation*. It is more than inclusion. Inclusion involves
imagining what is real for the client. Confirmation involves not
only seeing the client as he presently is, which may or may not be
acceptable, but also as he can be. Inclusion is necessary for the
occurrence of the therapeutic dialogue, but it is in the context of the
therapeutic dialogue that true confirmation occurs. Imagining
what was real for Jeffrey (inclusion) allowed me to feel what he felt.
I did not first seek an explanation of Jeffrey's reaction to his father
within my particular theoretical orientation but went directly to my
experience of him. The direct, unmediated sharing of Jeffrey's experience, as if it were my own, made an interpretation superfluous.

Confirmation of Jeffrey unfolded in the dialogue as the conversation focused on how he was affected by his experiences with
his father. We shared the consequence of the effect and he expressed
a desire to respond differently. In my own manner, I informed him
that this was an option that he was free to exercise if he wished to
do so, and I certainly supported his desire to change. In the context
of the dialogue, he felt empowered to change; as he and his wife
later indicated, he had indeed done so. The nurturing power of the
"between" created by the therapeutic dialogue had enabled Jeffrey
to make significant healing changes in his life and empowered me
to confirm the changes.

Client's Personal Direction as Guide for Confirmation

The therapist's confirmation of the client must always involve an
appreciation for the personal direction of the client's life—what is

right for the client. The therapist accepts the client but maintains an appreciation of what the client can be, and struggles with him to actualize his possibilities. The therapist's appreciation of the client's personal direction is not found in the therapist but in the between with the client. It emerges from what is created between them in their interactions with each other. I certainly felt that this was so in Jeffrey's case.

Case Examples

There are times when confirmation involves disapproval of the client's response because it is obviously not compatible with the personal direction of his life. I once had such a client—Jack. He was approaching his mid forties and having difficulties with his marriage. He presented himself as a man who placed high value on his contributions to society, clearly demonstrated in his history. His presenting problem was indecision about whether to end his marriage. He could not decide whether he should stay with his wife or leave her. Concurrently, he had developed a sexual relationship with another woman. I felt uncomfortable with his behavior, but I attributed my discomfort to the projection of my own values on Jack. I consoled myself that my function was to assist Jack in finding his way. Specifically, should he continue with his current wife or take up with another? After all, I had previously told him that I would not see his present wife unless it was for marital counseling and only if he made a commitment to try to repair the marriage. Thus, I felt my professional obligation was only to Jack.

In the session, he discussed his plans for the weekend. He would be spending it with his girlfriend while his wife was away. As the session progressed, I realized how caught up I was in Jack's experience. I was not comfortable and felt disturbed about his involvement with the other woman. I began to experience overwhelming feelings of anguish and despair. As I looked into Jack's face, I was compelled to say, "Are you sure you want to be with this woman this weekend? Is there not something within you that demands something better of you?" What in the world prompted me to make such a remark? I attribute it to the "enlightenment of the between." I was convinced, at that moment, that the client's decision was contrary to the personal direction of his life. In the next session, Jack stated that he had thought about what I had said and had decided I was right.

If pressed to analyze the reasons for my behavior, one could say what Jack was contemplating was so contrary to my own values that I simply could not tolerate it. As a therapist, I should never have imposed my personal values on Jack, for in doing so I was making the assumption that my reality was somehow more valid than his. I did not know what was best for him. Only he knew, and if he did not, it was not my prerogative to point it out to him. He must, in his therapeutic encounter with me, find it for himself.

From many therapists' point of view, the reason I should not have done what I did with Jack was obvious. It was contrary to my basic training not to accept the client always with unconditional positive regard. Yet, I had felt compelled to do it. Why? Because of the powerful effect of what had been created between Jack and me in our intimate interaction. It would have been a betrayal of my experience of Jack had I not admonished him as to the inappropriateness, for him, of his contemplated actions. Inappropriate for him, not because it was a breach of someone's morality, but because it was not compatible with the person whom I had come to know in our dialogue. In that moment, my concern for Jack was so intense that I could not tolerate silently standing by while he contemplated such a decision.

Confirmation demands that the therapist personally join in the client's struggle to be his best, to do what is right for himself with his whole being, to pursue the unique personal direction of his life as it unfolds in continuing dialogue. To do this, she must not distance herself from the client by assuming an objective stance, but she must be willing to accept the personal discomfort associated with the demands of the dialogue; for confirmation is not always approval. It may also involve confronting the client with one's disapproval. Whether it involves approval or disapproval, true confirmation is always a product of what is created between the therapist's and client's interaction and is in support of the client's personal direction.

That there can be no true confirmation without dialogue is illustrated in the case of Jerry. He was in his sixties, had been married for about twenty-eight years, and had a grown daughter.

Jerry had a career but was not happy with it and was in the process of changing to another. His presenting problem was his dissatisfaction with his career. He felt that the reason for his unhappiness was the way society viewed older men. As he explored this issue, he began to focus on his wife and her lack of interest in his concerns as the real source of his unhappiness. His wife was quite successful and was a high-level executive in her company. He felt her success was, in large part, due to his support and became increasingly angry as he explored this feeling. He then decided she was seeing another man and began checking the time she arrived home from work. He found that the time varied from day to day as much as ten minutes. He ruminated in his sessions as to what she was doing in these extra minutes, small as they were. In one of the ensuing sessions, he stated that it finally happened just as he knew it would; on the previous day she had taken twenty minutes longer getting home than she had on other days. He had confronted his wife in a fit of rage, totally perplexing her with his outburst.

Jerry had informed me in one of his previous sessions that he had hired a private investigator to check on his wife. The investigator had reported to him that his wife had left the office twenty minutes late on that day just as she had said. It seemed that this was one of those rare occasions when she had to complete a quarterly report and had to remain on the job until it was done. When she did not appear at her car on time to leave for home, the private investigator had gone inside the building and observed her at work in her office. He kept her under observation until she returned to her car and then followed her home noting that she was twenty minutes late. At the beginning of the session, Jerry informed me of the investigator's finding and asked if I would allow his wife to come in for the remainder of the session to discuss the matter. His wife joined us and much to my surprise he began the discussion by accusing her of stopping off on her way home to see her boyfriend. His wife protested her innocence to no avail. At this point, I asked his wife to leave. I then told him that what he was doing was demeaning to him and would not facilitate his quest for happiness. He informed me that I was bound by my professional confidentiality not to inform his wife and I would have to permit him to handle it the way he chose. I informed him that under such circumstances, I could no longer see him. I never saw Jerry again.

In the case of both Jack and Jerry, confirmation involved disapproval of what they were doing at that moment. However, for it to be true confirmation, such disapproval must unfold in the dialogue. In Jack's case, there was sufficient inclusion from me and responsiveness from him to generate a dialogue resulting in his acceptance of my disapproval. In other words, my disapproval was accepted by Jack because it unfolded in the interaction between us, resulting in true confirmation. Jack accepted my disapproval of his anticipated actions as caring rather than rejecting, and it was therefore healing rather than destructive.

This was not so in Jerry's case. My response to him did not come out of the dialogue. It came from my own sense of anger and indignation that he would make me an accomplice in his deception. At that moment, there was no attempt on my part to imagine what Jerry was thinking, how he perceived the situation, how he was feeling. There was no effort from my side of the relationship— inclusion—to share the deep hurt and disappointment that had driven him to such behavior. In that moment, I did not relate to Jerry's whole self. My interaction was with only with the bitter, angry, envious, and deceitful parts of him that had been severed from his unified wholeness, thus precluding a dialogue.

Summation and Preview

Before leaving our discussion of confirmation, let us review certain pragmatic concerns. The therapist must, in her interactions with the client, be fully present and in direct contact with him. She must allow herself without preconception or interpretation to feel, think, and perceive like the client by imagining what is real for him in that moment. Finally, she must be willing to place herself in harm's way by accepting the burden and pain of the client's psychic state. When she has accomplished these concerns, she has offered the client the gift of inclusion. If the client is able to accept the therapist's inclusion, there is an interaction, a therapeutic dialogue, that may produce a new reality between them. In the context of this reality, both the therapist and the client are empowered to respond in ways that were not previously available to either. The therapist's utilization of confirmation is most appropriate in those moments during the therapy session when this occurs.

When we interact with another in such a way as to impose our own wishes and desires on him without regard for his unique wholeness, we are existentially guilty. We have injured the order of the human world we know and recognize as our own. In those instances in which the other imposes his wishes and desires on us without regard for our unique wholeness, we may experience neurotic guilt. The implications of these two expressions of guilt—existential and neurotic—in our life are discussed in the following chapter.

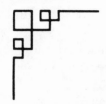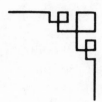

12

Existential
Guilt

All of us have the ability to set something at a distance and relate
to it, allowing us to share a common world. We use this ability
when we set at a distance another human being and relate as an
independent person to another like us. Our innate ability to speak
with meaning to each other allows us to share a world built on all
mankind's present and past conversations (I–It relations) and com-
munions (I–Thou relations). These common abilities, to distance
and relate and speak with meaning, make it possible for us to share
our individual existence with each other and thus create what Buber
has called a common order among humans across the generations
(Buber, 1988, p. 117).

   We measure the appropriateness of our conduct toward each
other by this common order. We are born into it and contribute to
it throughout the course of our life, whether for its good or bad.
Because of our inherent relational nature, we cannot develop or
thrive as whole beings without participating in this common order.
The extent to which we respond, whether in a constructive or an
injurious manner, determines the measure of our humanness. Ex-

istential guilt arises when we, by our personal action or lack of action, injure this common order (Buber, 1988, p. 117).

It is the "I" of oneself that experiences the guilt since the injury is the result of one's conscious activities. The "I" has the ability not only to distance from and reflect upon one's environment but also to reflect upon oneself. Since our I emerges out of the very ground of our being and is inalienable to us, it also has the ability to synthesize its reflections on our conscious activities and evaluate them. This ability is commonly referred to as the work of the conscience—the capacity to distinguish between our past and future actions that should and should not be approved. Included are acts of omission as well commission. Thus, existential guilt is a conscious experience.

Threefold Resolution of Existential Guilt

Buber has told us that to resolve existential guilt we must respond to it in a threefold action. "First, to illuminate the darkness that still weaves itself about the guilt despite all the previous action of the conscience—not to illuminate it with a spotlight but a broad, enduring wave of light" (Buber, 1988, p. 126). The metaphor of illumination is used to emphasize the need for one's complete awareness of the source of the injury. The light is a broad wave and not a spotlight to emphasize the nature of the awareness. Such light does not allow for shadows in which the residual of irresponsible denial or rationalization may lurk. If there is to be a resolution of the injury we have done, there must be no attempt, not even a partial one, to cover our responsibility. The awareness is thorough and complete and involves the whole self. Also notice in the metaphor that the light is enduring. In order to resolve our existential guilt, we must persevere in this uncomfortable state until the work has been completed.

Buber has said the person's action is "to persevere, no matter how high he may have ascended in his present life above that station of guilt—to persevere in the newly won humble knowledge of the identity of the present person with the person of that time" (Buber, 1988, p. 126). We must acknowledge that it was "I" who effected the injury and no other. It is "I" who currently exist and who also existed as I at the time of the injury and no other who is responsible. I cannot say it was a part of myself that no longer exists that was responsible—for example, I was a youngster, I was immature, I was under great stress, I was beside myself, I was not thinking, I just went along with the crowd, I am now not that kind of person. I must acknowledge with my whole self, including all I have been and all I am to become, that I am responsible. The excessive amount of psychic energy utilized in defending against such action drains us and results in fragmentation and loss of future possibilities for being. In this sense, the injury not only hurts the other but limits our own existence as well.

Buber has said that the final and third action is for a person "in his place and according to his capacity, in the given historical and biographical situation, to restore the order-of-being injured by him through the relation of an active devotion to the world—for the wounds of the order-of-being can be healed in infinitely many other places than those at which they were inflicted" (Buber, 1988, p. 126). The passage of time precludes an undoing of what has been done. The event in which the injury occurred cannot be recalled and the person involved is often no longer available. In such cases, we must turn our efforts to other relations in the world to heal the injury. The completion of the work is to be found in our active and devoted commitment to future relations with the world, for the injury is to the common order of humans. It is an injury to the between that exists in all authentic human relationships and in this sense is an injury to all humans both present and future.

The unwillingness to experience the discomfort of the three-fold action of resolving existential guilt may cause us to attempt to remove it from our consciousness. But because of its ontic nature, it does not dissipate but remains in our existence. We can resolve it only by going through the unpleasant state of illumination, acceptance, and reconciliation, which are the prerequisites to restoring the injured order. We must give up control to a reality that lies beyond us, to be probed and guided by the between of the relation we have injured. The condemnation comes from beyond us. It comes from the between of our interaction with the other in the injured relation.

Neurotic Guilt

Neurotic guilt arises when we take responsibility for an injury to ourselves that has been imposed on us by an other. The injury results from the other's expectations of us, a condition that has nothing to do with what we are intended to be but rather what the other expects us to be. Although we accept responsibility for the injury to the relationship, we are not responsible. It is the other who is responsible. Since our feelings of guilt do not stem from our injury of the relationship, they are groundless. They are the results of demands and expectations imposed on us by our family or society. Once the source of the neurotic guilt feelings is consciously identified and accepted, the feelings tend to dissipate for there is no real guilt.

Importance of Distinguishing Two Kinds of Guilt

Because of the basic differences between existential and neurotic guilt, the therapist should take care to discern which type of guilt the client presents. When the guilt is neurotic, the therapist's task is to assist the client in alleviating his feelings, for there is no "real" guilt.

In existential guilt, the therapist's task is to support the client in its resolution. The therapist must support the need of the client to persevere as he goes through the unpleasant states of illumination, acceptance, and reconciliation, which are necessary to alleviate the guilt. The therapist must be willing to be with him in his illumination and not attempt to remove his uncomfortable feelings of guilt; she must support and respect his efforts to resolve his guilt for existential guilt permeates us totally and cannot be relieved by removing it from our awareness.

Case Examples

An example of existential guilt is a man who appeared at my office after a driving while drinking violation. He owned his own business, he was married, and he had four children. His presenting problem was his feelings of shame and guilt after receiving a citation for driving under the influence of alcohol. After attending a local business conference, he had had several drinks with friends. Then, on his way home he ran into an automobile with several people in it. Fortunately, no one was injured, but the experience had been frightening. He was arrested and charged with driving while under the influence.

Several weeks later, he appeared at my office. He complained of not being able to sleep at night or concentrate during the day because of his deep feelings of shame and guilt over what he had done. Often as he spoke, this large, muscular man wept without restraint. He spoke of how he had betrayed his relationship to his company, his family, and himself. He stated that he could find no way to escape from the shame and guilt of what he had done. I realized that I was in the presence of a man suffering from profound existential guilt. His feelings of guilt were not neurotic; he was truly guilty. It would have been disrespectful of his potential to say, "Come on now, a lot of people have drunk a little too much and driven their cars. It is not as if you intended to have a wreck. It could happen to anyone. Stop feeling so bad." In such cases, the client does not need the therapist to be supportive. It is the guilt feelings themselves that the self uses to accomplish its task of reconciliation and healing. To be supportive means to accept and understand the process the client must go through for healing to occur.

I explained to the man the process he was experiencing and suggested that he try to assess where his feelings of shame and guilt were taking him: what was his shame and guilt trying to accomplish in him? He was perplexed and said he did not understand. I explained that he knew why he felt guilty but did not seem to know what he was supposed to do about it. What if the intent of such guilt feelings was to motivate him to accomplish some type of reconciliation? He asked what I thought this could be. I explained that it was a matter for him to discover, for in the discovery, his healing would begin. In no way did I try to alleviate his feelings of guilt.

At the next session, he was relieved and reported that he had been thinking about what he was supposed to do with his feelings of guilt. He indicated that he had been led to reestablish his relationship with his children. He had discussed his problem with his wife and now felt much closer to her. His friends had accepted his apology for his behavior and had assured him that the incident would not affect his standing with them. He reported feeling much closer to his family and more responsible to his friends. He had accomplished the threefold action of illumination, perseverance, and reconciliation and was no longer overwhelmed by feelings of guilt and shame.

Often the guilt the client is experiencing is neurotic in nature. I once treated a man who was a corporate executive in a large company. Gene seemed to have everything. The corporation he worked for was a success; he had a loving wife, three fine children, and a beautiful home in an exclusive, closed community. However, he was always in trouble because he never seemed to follow through on his deals. His wife complained that she was constantly having to push him to finish what he had started. She had become frustrated by his behavior and insisted that he get help.

Gene asked me to help him stop procrastinating. He said he could not figure out why he did it. After several sessions, I began to understand his dilemma. He had struggled as a youngster to make contact with his father who was an alcoholic. He was killed in a fight in a bar while he was intoxicated. Gene always felt that if only he had been a good enough son, his father would have stopped drinking; but no matter how hard he tried, his father did not change.

In a later session, Gene remembered that at some point in his earlier life he had decided he was a failure and did not deserve success. Consequently, at this time in his life, as he was becoming increasingly aware of his success, he felt the increasing urge to "goof off." He described it as an ambivalent experience. A part of him wanted to succeed, yet another part of him felt he did not deserve success. He stated that the more successful he became, the more guilty he felt.

In the course of Gene's treatment, the repressed source of his guilt feelings was recalled and made conscious. As he became aware of and consciously examined the source of the guilt feelings, he was able to see the inappropriateness of his assumed guilt for his father's drinking and subsequent death. This realization in its fullness negated his guilt feelings.

It is not uncommon to see both existential and neurotic guilt present, as in Joe, a client in his early twenties. His presenting problem was cocaine addiction and marital discord. He had lost his job and could not find another. This state had created a great hardship for him and his family. His relationship with his wife had been deeply injured by his drug abuse and she was very frightened for the welfare of the family. Her way of handling the situation was to monitor her husband's activities by constant inquiries. His response was anger and resentment. The content of their conversation consisted of something like, "Joe, what are you going to do? We have no money for food for the children. The rent is due this week. What do I tell the landlord? When are you going to find work?" Joe's response was usually, "I don't know Sue, I just don't know. What in the hell do you want me to do? I'm doing the best I can." It was in this context his session with me occurred.

During the session, Joe discussed the possibility of asking his mother for assistance. Sue turned to Joe and pleaded with him not to do it. Seeing Joe's increasing frustration and anger, she asked that he try to understand how she felt. As she wept she spoke of Joe being gone for days at a time when he was addicted. She spoke of her fear and concern for his safety and her feelings of desperation as she realized she could do nothing. When she could stand it no longer, she had called Joe's mother for help. Joe's mother had refused her. In Sue's mind, Joe's mother had shown no concern for her own grandchildren. She talked of how deeply she had been hurt by his mother's rejection. She did not want Joe to do or say anything to his mother about the matter. She only wanted Joe to understand how badly his mother had hurt her. She repeatedly asked Joe if he would please try to understand. She stated that if he just gave her that much, she could tolerate their situation. Finally, Joe burst out in a rage, "You will not talk about my mother! You have never liked her! I won't have you criticizing her!"

As I watched this conversation unfold, I realized that Joe could not respond to Sue's requests for understanding until he dealt with both his neurotic and existential guilt. In previous sessions, Joe and Sue had given me enough information regarding Joe's mother for me to conclude that Joe did not feel he had lived up to his mother's expectations. The mother's love for Joe was conditional: everything was all right as long as Joe did what she wanted.

When he did not, his mother withdrew her love. It was evident that Joe could not acknowledge how badly his mother had hurt Sue until he acknowledged how badly his mother had hurt him. He had handled this hurt by assuming that he, not his mother, was at fault. For not attaining his mother's standards, he was experiencing neurotic guilt. Although the mother was the guilty one, Joe had assumed the responsibility and was experiencing guilt feelings. Until he acknowledged and alleviated these neurotic conditions, it would be impossible for Joe to understand how badly his mother had treated his wife and children.

The situation was further compounded by Joe's existential guilt, having injured his relationship with his wife and children. Joe had not, for whatever reasons, been willing to face the threefold action necessary to resolve his existential guilt. In this instance, Joe did not just *feel* guilty; he *was* guilty. This is an issue that often is not brought up in therapy because of the commonly accepted notion that chemical abuse is a disease. The disease concept can be used to alleviate personal responsibility for using, although this is certainly not seen in the steps of the Narcotics Anonymous Program. For Joe to understand the hurt Sue suffered when she was abandoned by his mother, he must also acknowledge his own abandonment of Sue and work out his existential guilt. Healing will not occur until he has accomplished this.

Summation and Preview

To summarize, the source of neurotic guilt is usually hidden from the client. It stems from the client's being injured by another (family or society) but assuming responsibility as if he had injured the other. Ontically speaking, the client is not guilty but he experiences guilt feelings as if he were. When the client becomes aware of his erroneous acceptance of the responsibility for the injury, he can alleviate his guilt feelings without impairing his existence. This is not true for existential guilt.

Because of the ontic nature of existential guilt, the therapist must always be attuned to the source of the client's guilt. If the client has personally injured a relationship that is contrary to the nature of his existence, either by omission or commission, then he is existentially guilty. In such cases, the therapist must point this out and stand with the client without interfering as he goes through the process of illumination, acceptance, and reconciliation. This work cannot be accomplished by removing the client's feelings of guilt. It requires that the therapist accept and respect the client's ability to accomplish the work; it is something he cannot and must not do for the client. It is a work that only the client can do, for it is in the threefold process that existential guilt accomplishes its work in the existence of the client.

There is a unique personal reality that we take from the dialogue that is embodied in us and becomes part of our ongoing existence. It is this reality—what we have acquired in our past dialogues—that we take to future dialogues. This reality is constantly being reshaped and elaborated in each succeeding dialogue. Friedman (1972, 1985) refers to this unique and dynamic personal reality as our *dialogue of touchstones*. The significance of our touchstones will be discussed in the following chapter.

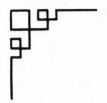

13

Touchstones

Each of us is capable of I-Thou relationships with others in the world. Each instance of such relating brings into existence a new reality found between us in our interaction. Friedman refers to this experience as "touchstones of reality" and as the "dialogue of touchstones" when it unfolds in our dialogue with others (Friedman, 1985). Our touchstones carry the effect of the dialogue and remain with us. Thus each of us possesses our own unique touchstones created when we encounter others in dialogue.

The Reality of the Between

Our touchstones are derived from the reality of the between and are experienced by us totally. Our experience of subjective and objective reality is limited to our conscious parts. Outside of dialogue, our

This section is based on private conversations with Maurice Friedman and on selections from his books, *The Healing Dialogue in Psychotherapy* (1985), Chapter 18, and *Touchstones of Reality: Existential Trust and the Community of Peace* (1972), Chapter 1.

subjective reality is available only to us individually. Objective reality is a public experience, arrived at through general consensus. In spite of differences in the ways we experience subjective and objective realities, they share a common characteristic that is not found in the touchstones of dialogue. Our experience of subjective and objective reality is based on the apperception of our inner and outer sensations and perceptions. These two types of reality are consciously experienced through acts of apperception or reflection. They are mediated rather than being immediate and direct. They are always experienced after being processed by the individual and the group or the society in which we exist. This is not so with our touchstones. With them, the experience is immediate and direct. It affects us totally and in a manner different from either subjective or objective reality. It can be *apprehended* but not comprehended.

It is in our openness to the encounter with another that our touchstones evolve and we find our unique direction. Buber (1965b, p. 68) warns us of attempting to anticipate before the situation what we will do. We must wait for the answer, which comes in the situation and not before. Our touchstones are constantly being shaped and changed by our dialogical encounters with others. There can be no certainty before the event as to what will be called out since each concrete event is unique.

Evolutionary Nature of Touchstones

Touchstones, once experienced, remain latent in a basic layer of ourselves until they reveal themselves to us in a concrete way, that is, when they are called out in a future dialogue. At that time, these unique touchstones are redefined into something that has never occurred before and will never occur again. As each touchstone is shaped by dialogue, it builds on and elaborates the previous dialogue's effect. The direction of our life unfolds in this flow of changes in touchstones.

The therapist may conclude that since the client's touchstones have a historical development, they can be used to predict the future direction of the client's life. This is deceptive. Such a prediction would be based on the certainty that the past would occur again in the future, and this is not so. The direction of the client's life is not static or predictable. It is constantly unfolding in the dialogue.

It is possible also to have a dialogue with our touchstones that have emerged from previous dialogues. These can be normal day-to-day dialogues of touchstones with friends or therapeutic dialogues of touchstones between therapist and client.

When two people in ordinary daily dialogue share their touchstones, there is no need to determine who is right. A true understanding and appreciation of touchstones eliminates the necessity for one side or the other to be right or wrong. Each has his own unique sense of reality and his touchstones for him are true. The basic logical principle of the excluded middle (everything is either A or not A) does not apply. For each, his touchstones reflect his own unique sense of reality.

When each brings his touchstones to the dialogue, there is a fusion in the between that alters and creates new touchstones for each. These new touchstones would not have come into existence without sharing in the dialogue the differences of the other's touchstones. If we are open to such dialogues, our touchstones are constantly being reshaped to accommodate the differences in others. Such openness demands that we not commit ourselves to a reality that is preconceived. We must remain open to the uncertainty of the dialogue wherever it takes us. The reality of the between that unfolds in the dialogue is not predictable or preordained. It is a reality found only as we go out to meet others. It is in our meeting with others that we experience the confirmation of our uniqueness and pursue our life's personal direction, thus moving beyond ourselves to become more. The ordinary dialogue is mutual in that each participant has such experiences and is changed by the life stance of the other.

The therapeutic dialogue between the therapist and the client is not mutual in all respects. There is mutual contact, trust, and concern between the therapist and the client, but there is not mutual inclusiveness. Inclusion comes only from the therapist's side of the dialogue.

Touchstones as Essence of the Individual

The client brings to the therapeutic dialogue his own unique circumstances, which have made him ill. His touchstones have been so unacceptable to others that he has not been confirmed. This has presented him with a dilemma. If he has denied the reality of his touchstones, he has been separated from his sense of real being as a person. On the other hand, if he has not been accepted, he has not been able to relate to others and in this sense has been cut off from the community. In either case, he has experienced a profound sense of alienation, which has disturbed him.

The therapist brings her touchstones into the therapeutic dialogue to effect healing in the client. Her touchstones are no more valid than the client's, but they bring experience and expertise in imagining the real, inclusion, and confirmation; these can be used to raise the client's touchstones from the realm of I to We, and thus overcome his alienation.

It is within the therapeutic dialogue of touchstones that the dialogical psychotherapist works to heal the client's disturbed self. The therapist may have the skill and knowledge to participate but not to direct the course of the client's healing. It is a humbling experience that calls forth the uniqueness of both the client and therapist.

The dialogical psychotherapist is interested in the client's acquisition of touchstones as well as his response to them. Since our touchstones are the substance of what we retain from the dialogue, any hindrance to their acquisition is an obstacle to the dialogue. As obstacles to dialogue are discussed in Chapter Fourteen, hindrances are not dealt with here. I will, however, present clinical examples to illustrate what happens when our actual life stance is not compatible with our touchstones and the self becomes fragmented and disturbed. When our life stance and our touchstones are compatible, we are in the process of becoming what we are intended to be as human beings.

Case Examples

Often the client presenting an unauthentic life stance comes from a background in which he was not confirmed when he was authentic. The only way he could gain confirmation was to assume a life stance incompatible with his touchstones. Therefore, he has lived seeming to be what others want him to be rather than what he was intended to be. Some time ago, I counseled a person who had experienced such confirmation from his community. Manuel was single, had never married, had no children, and had been a heroin addict for several years. I worked with Manuel to assist him in breaking the habit. On three occasions, he was sent to the hospital to detoxify, only to return to drugs. After undergoing his third detoxification, Manuel's colleagues decided to offer their support. All of them had watched Manuel struggle with his addiction and had learned to care for him. They organized themselves into watchers. Each took a time of day or night to be with Manuel. One of them was with him every hour of the day. For several weeks after Manuel's release, this watching continued until it was apparent that Manuel had broken his addiction. While his friends' watching was occurring, Manuel had come to me with tears in his eyes and said, "I've never been cared for like this in my life. I don't understand why they are doing it." I told him it was because they were concerned that he succeed at his job.

Several months later, Manuel came to me and announced his intention to resign from his job. I was amazed and spoke to him of my surprise. I told him how proud his colleagues were of his progress. He had stayed with the job and conquered his drug addiction. I asked, "Why do you want to quit now? You are a success. Everyone admires you for what you have done and your job is secure." He responded: "You people have really fucked with my head, man. When I showed up on this job, I knew who I was—a junkie. Now you have made me a straight dude. I'm lost, man. I don't know how to be straight. I only know how to be a junkie. I've been a junkie all my adult life. I'm going back to the streets where I know who I am." With that, Manuel left a good-paying job where he was respected and cared for to return to a life that was not authentic but one that was familiar to him.

It was almost three years later that Manuel spoke to me on the phone. I asked what he was doing. He laughed and said, "You thought I was back on the streets using. Man, I could never go back to that after what happened there with me. I'm clean and working in a community program for junkies like I used to be." His attempts at seeming no longer worked. The dialogue that had unfolded in the concern of his fellow workers had left him with touchstones that were unshakable.

In other cases, the client has found that the uncertainty associated with an openness to the unknown, which is necessary for the pursuit of one's personal direction, is too uncomfortable to tolerate. It has been easier to allow another to provide the direction in his life. Such a person may go through life waiting for others to do for him what only he can do if lasting change in his life is to occur. But, for him, it is more expedient to continue manipulating others to do the work than to experience the discomfort of arousal that accompanies the self's preparation for such tasks.

Carolyn was such a client. She was sixty-seven years of age when she appeared in my office. She was married and had six children, all of whom were married and had children of their own. Carolyn had eleven grandchildren. She had worked all her life and had retired at the age of sixty-five. Since retirement, she had been in constant conflict with her husband. He complained that she was driving him crazy. She was always hanging around him, wanting him to tell her what she should do. She took no responsibility for planning or doing anything. Her presenting problem was boredom. She stated that she had nothing to live for now that she had retired. While she was working, there had been a routine to follow and things to do. Now there was nothing.

Although Carolyn had a large family, she had very little meaningful involvement with them. By her own admission, she was too absorbed by her dilemma to enjoy her grandchildren. She insisted that her husband was the problem. He would not help her. When I asked how he should help her, she replied, "You know, Doctor, do things with me like we used to do when I was working. Everything has changed now; all he wants me to do is to clean the house so he can do his work. There is nothing meaningful for me to do and even when I do have something to do, it doesn't seem to help. Why can't he be more considerate and help me to find something I can do with myself?"

Each activity I suggested was met by "Yes, but." Several sessions later, as I struggled with Carolyn's unwillingness to accept responsibility, she suddenly blurted out, "When I was a girl, my mother always told me what to do. When I was working, I knew what to do. If I didn't, someone was always around to tell me." I watched as Carolyn, in a fit of rage and anger, demanded that I help her. She then apologized for her outburst, stating she had no right to demand that I get involved. Her husband was the problem. It was evident that Carolyn was waiting for someone to do for her what only she could do if she was to live an authentic life. Until her retirement, Carolyn had depended on others to determine her life's personal direction. It may not have been the most meaningful life, but it was safe, and it spared her the uncertainty associated with pursuing what she was intended to be. She had avoided the mystery of her unique potential, but as a result she was a very frightened woman who was convinced her life was totally without meaning unless it was provided by others.

In still other cases, the client has learned to avoid the mystery of becoming through activity. He avoids pursuit of his life's personal direction by responding to events in an indiscriminate manner, depending on how he feels at that moment. He is pulled this way and that in a flurry of activity without regard for direction. He is unable to be decisive, to use his passions in pursuing his life's personal direction.

Jeff was such a client. He was married and had no children. He had barely finished high school and currently worked as a maintenance man for a local company. He described himself as a ne'er-do-well who had done little with his life besides surf, drink, smoke pot, and chase women. He had married for expediency. His wife wanted to marry, she had a tight little body, was good in bed, and never demanded anything of him.

His presenting problem was an affair he was having with a young woman who had a tight little body like his wife used to have but didn't have any more. At this point, he apologized for his need to have a tight body. His wife had always been supportive, but she shouldn't have gotten fat. He stated, "That's just the way I am and I can't help it. I feel bad about it." He then asked, "Should I leave my wife and take up with this new woman? I've been with my old lady for the last twelve years and, Doc, to make things worse, she has begun nagging me for a baby. She is getting older and wants to start a family. The last thing I want in my life is the responsibility of a kid."

As the session progressed, it became obvious that Jeff was fighting depression. He continued to describe himself as a man who had always done whatever felt best to him at the time. If he did not feel like going to work, he stayed home and surfed and drank with his buddies. Lately, this way of living was not making him happy. He stated that he must be going through his mid-life crisis or something and needed to settle down. He spoke of how difficult it was for him and how life had become "a bitch." Life for him just wasn't fun any more. When he discussed what he would have to go through to change his life-style, he became very despondent. He did not feel he could change because that was just the way he was. Yet, he could not believe that what he was doing was all life had to offer him. I watched as he struggled to maintain his composure. He appeared like a frightened child who had suddenly realized that there was more to life than just doing whatever he felt like doing. He left the session shaken by his realization, protesting that he just couldn't change, yet understanding that he could never be all he was intended to be without change. He was a man struggling not to be responsive to his touchstones by filling his life with meaningless activity.

In yet other cases, the client may attempt to avoid the mystery associated with the pursuit of his personal direction by an obsession with certainty. Such a person finds his safety in sameness and constantly struggles to make certain that nothing unusual enters his life. He is always selecting and focusing on what he is accustomed to, excluding what is different. To ensure this sameness in his life, he must be unresponsive to his touchstones. To the extent that he is successful, his life is safe but not authentic.

Judd's presenting problem was marital discord resulting from his unemployment. His wife believed that his inability to find employment was affecting his self-esteem. She complained that they no longer made love and that he was very withdrawn and uncommunicative. One of her major concerns was his drinking. Judd drank as many as twelve beers a day and had been told by his doctor to quit after his heart attack, which had occurred several years ago. In response to her complaints, Judd contended that he had always been shy and was not a social butterfly. As for his beer drinking, she knew he drank before she married him and he was not going to change his habits for her or anyone else.

As the sessions progressed, it became evident that Judd was

very rigid. He pursued a daily routine that he would not break. He always got up at the same time, no earlier and no later. He kept his things in a certain place and no one was to remove them or rearrange them. His wife complained that his rigidity was driving her nuts. He was totally devoid of spontaneity. If you asked him a simple question, he would pause for long periods of time before answering. You could see him struggling with his answer. When I asked him what was happening when this occurred, he replied, "I just want to be sure I answer correctly."

Later, Judd had a job offer; however, he did not know whether he could accept since it would involve doing things he had never done before. He wrestled with this dilemma for several sessions. He finally decided to try the job but soon became deeply disturbed because his work was not accurate. When his wife explained that's the way the work had been done since its inception, Judd responded with anger and said that he would be no part of something he did not know for certain was right. When I challenged him to fix it, since he was a bright man, he became very uncomfortable and indicated that he could not do that since he could not predict how it would turn out. Judd's avoidance of uncertainty was a recurring theme in the therapy sessions.

His intolerance of uncertainty was seen in his and his wife's preparation for a visit with friends in another state. Before Judd would consent to go, his wife had to agree on what they would do in each situation as it arose; for example, what they would tell people about themselves at the dinner table. Judd stated emphatically that he wanted no surprises. When they went to a dance, she must be certain to protect him from other women asking him to dance. She also had to agree not to ask him to dance more than twice. He then defined the type of music that must be playing before they danced. They must never enter the dance floor before there were at least three other couples dancing. The details of the planning went on and on. It became increasingly obvious as the treatment progressed that Judd was unable to respond to his touchstones because of his need for certainty in his life. There is no way one's uniqueness can unfold without the ability to tolerate uncertainty. Judd utilized his intellect to avoid growth—to avoid experiencing something he had never experienced before. He was trading the

predictability of sameness for the enigma of becoming what he was
intended to be.

Before leaving our discussion of touchstones in therapy, let
us look at one more example that illustrates how the therapeutic
dialogue shapes and elaborates one's touchstones. Carl was married
and had four daughters all living at home. He had been a manager
of a furniture store when his employer had been engaged in tax
fraud. Carl said the man had duped him into signing certain papers
that facilitated the movement of unreported funds. Although he had
been innocent of any intent to do wrong, he had been found guilty
of tax fraud along with his employer. As he awaited sentencing by
the court, Carl came to see me because of the anxiety that his con-
viction had precipitated.

In the initial sessions, Carl was bitter and cynical. He constantly complained of the unfairness of his situation and how no
one understood. He was unable to secure a loan from his friends to
ensure the well-being of his wife and daughter while he was in
prison. In his mind, no one cared what happened to him and his
family, not even God. He contended that he had been a practicing
Catholic and had prayed to God for help. He asked, "If God is the
most powerful being there is, how come the world has so many
problems?" Throughout most of his initial sessions, he appeared
confused and bewildered by his circumstances. He seemed unable to
make sense of what had happened to him. He saw the world as cruel
and rejecting. Even God had turned His back on him.

I began to see that my task was to engage Carl in dialogue
so that his perception of reality, his touchstones, might be changed.
As I struggled to understand how he felt—inclusion—he became
increasingly more responsive to my suggestions that there were
other ways to view his situation. As we began to explore what had
happened, Carl was able to look at the mistake he had made in
signing the papers for his employer. He became more open and
acknowledged his culpability. We then began dealing with how he
was going to handle his situation. I pointed out the inevitability of
his imprisonment and his inability to change the situation. At one
time, as we were discussing his helplessness, he asked in a pleading
manner, "Doc, what can I do?" It was at this point I suggested that
the only thing he had any control over was the way he responded

to the situation, and that this would involve his looking at it from a different perspective—in dialogical terms, to alter his touchstones of reality.

In subsequent sessions, I joined with Carl in his struggle to alter his touchstones. I suggested that since he had to go through it, the least he could do was to try to find some meaning and purpose in the dilemma, his personal direction. It was in this context that from time to time Carl and I engaged in dialogue, and I began to see a change in his attitude. He stated, "Doc, my situation has not changed, and I still don't know how I'm going to handle it, but somehow I feel different." He was able to see that maybe God had not abandoned him but just expected him to do his part in facing the situation. In subsequent sessions he was accepting of this situation and open to the changes it was going to produce in his life. He stated that he was still anxious but no longer felt bitter and cynical. His touchstones had been altered in the dialogue.

Summation and Preview

Throughout the course of therapy, as the therapist and the client engage in dialogue, not only do they share their respective touchstones, but the touchstones of both are altered. However, in the therapeutic dialogue, the concern is focused on changes in the client's touchstones. At times, the changes are subtle and evolve slowly. At other times, the changes are dramatic and extensive. The examples I have presented are striking and may not always be typical, but they illustrate how the client's touchstones are shaped and elaborated in dialogue with the therapist.

This discussion by no means exhausts all the possible ways in which the client may avoid responding authentically to his touchstones nor how his touchstones may be shaped and elaborated in the dialogue; however, it is sufficient for our purposes. Regardless of the manner in which the dialogue occurs, the therapist must take care not to impose herself on the client. She must not present her opinions and attitudes so as to make the client feel that she is speaking from his insight rather than her own. She must respect the client's ability to unfold in the dialogue by actually being with him as he goes through the process of becoming. It is a work—the client's authentic response to his touchstones of reality—that can be accomplished by the client only in dialogue with the therapist.

Touchstones of reality is the term first used by Maurice Friedman to designate the substance of the dialogue that is retained, stored, and constantly shaped as each succeeding dialogue occurs. He later referred to it as *touchstones of dialogue.* An understanding of our touchstones, which emerge from dialogue, and their subsequent expression in dialogue is crucial to the dialogical psychotherapist. The dialogue of touchstones is the culmination and expression of what comes to us from the between.

In Part Two, which follows, we begin to explore the clinical applications of the eleven elements of dialogical psychotherapy that have been presented in Part One.

PART TWO

Clinical Considerations and Dialogical Psychotherapy

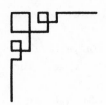 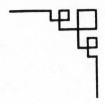

14

The Therapeutic
Dialogue

In this chapter we examine the therapeutic implications of the elements that have been presented. We look at their clustering into constellations that are the basic tools of the dialogical psychotherapist and how these can be used to heal the client. Martin Buber has said that had he been born in another time, perhaps the Middle Ages, he might have been more concerned with the neglect of our I–It relations with the world. However, at this time in our history, our scientific and technological advances make such concern no longer necessary. It is the neglect of the Thou in the world that was his concern. Such neglect has resulted in our personal selves becoming sick. Healing can only come from our refocusing on the Thou (private conversation between Buber and Maurice Friedman, Sept. 1951).

The Client as Unique

To help with the client's healing the dialogical therapist must relate to the client as Thou. As each person is unique, our experience of him or her can only be apprehended, never totally comprehended. This approach may be in conflict with the past experience of the therapist who has been trained to be analytical. The skills we use to effect analytical comprehension require a method for separating out the parts of the whole and noting their connections, but in the therapeutic dialogue we must relate to the person in his or her totality.

To see the client as a whole person, the therapist must celebrate the client's uniqueness and realize that no one like him or her will ever be created again. The client has potentials that will never be found in any other person. Only the client can realize them. The therapist must see the client as someone of inestimable value; for the time they are together in the therapeutic endeavor, the client is worthy of his total regard. The client's welfare is the focus of his entire concern. The therapist must strive to be totally present and focused on the client's concerns. The therapist brings his whole undivided self to the interaction. If the therapist has the ability to share himself in this manner with the client, there is the possibility of a healing dialogue.

Inclusion

In such moments of sharing, when the therapist is totally focused on the client and his worth, the therapist may initiate inclusion if he is willing to experience the client in a direct and real manner. Inclusion is accomplished when the therapist is able to imagine what is real for the client, to imagine with his whole being and without distraction or reservation what the client is willing, thinking, feeling, and perceiving at that moment. He must focus on what is real for the client, without consideration for his own comfort. He must experience the exact same psychic state of the client, regardless of the pain, as his own. At the same time, he is aware of himself as a person separate and different from the client.

When the therapist accomplishes this type of intimate interaction with the client, inclusion occurs from his side of the relationship. At that moment when the client is willing to accept the therapist's inclusion and to believe that the concern of the therapist is authentic, a dialogue may take place. For such a dialogue to occur, there must be mutual and simultaneous participation by both partners, except for inclusion, which comes only from the therapist. When this type of intimate interaction actually occurs, the therapist and client are engaged in a therapeutic dialogue. Because of the nature of this interaction, its locus is removed from either of the partners to what is created between them. It is in this new reality between them that they truly speak with meaning to each other and the healing work is done in the meeting.

Barriers to Dialogue

The therapeutic dialogue can be created only by the mutual and simultaneous participation of the client and the therapist. It is a phenomenon that lies between both and cannot be created by either alone. Although both share it, neither can create it or control it. In this section, we will discuss some of the barriers to the dialogue.

Objectivity of Therapist

As therapists, most of us have been trained to approach our clients in a warm and personable manner but always to maintain our objectivity. Usually, we use only a part of ourselves to interact with the client in an accepting and understanding manner while with another part we are observing what is going on in the interaction. For the observing part not to be overwhelmed and cluttered, we must observe selectively and arrange what we see. To interpret our observations we impose a theoretical grid on what we observe—that is, we adopt a particular theoretical orientation that serves as a guide to show us what is important. That which does not fit is usually ignored since its relevance to our particular theoretical orientation is not considered important. The traditional participant/observer role of the therapist means that the therapist is divided in relating to the client. One part must observe while another part interacts. He cannot commit his whole, undivided self to the therapeutic interaction. In addition, his contact with the client is not direct but mediated. He has contact with only that part of the client that has been strained through his theoretical grid.

The therapist's struggle to be objective is not unlike that of any other scientist who develops a particular methodology that allows him to attend selectively to those aspects of a particular phenomenon he considers important. He then imposes his theoretical formulations on this selection to generalize to other similar phenomena that he has not studied. The dialogical psychotherapist certainly does not discount such endeavors. However, to the extent that the therapist maintains an observing stance with the client (I-It), he cannot share the client's real world in which there are no generalities but only a uniquely concrete existence.

Skilled therapists from different orientations are more similar to one another in their approach to therapy than they are to less skilled therapists from their own orientations. The more skilled we become in the practice of inclusion and subsequent dialogue with the client, the less we tend to rely on a particular theoretical orientation. This does not mean that the therapist must discard his theoretical orientation to practice dialogical psychotherapy. However, he should be aware that it can be an obstacle to the therapeutic dialogue.

Realistically, what usually happens in the therapeutic process is that the therapist moves back and forth from inclusion and dialogue (I-Thou) to observation and analysis (I-It). However, the dialogical psychotherapist understands that the real work of healing occurs in the therapeutic dialogue. This does not mean that other interactions with the client do not have benefits. They enable him to discuss with himself and other therapists of like mind what he thinks is happening with the patient and to make plans for coping with it and thus reduce the uncertainty associated with the therapeutic process. They make it possible for him to generalize his experience from one client to another. They enable the development of a body of knowledge that may be drawn on to inform and train other therapists. But they do not facilitate dialogue with the client.

Therapist's Stereotyping of Clients

Certain personal characteristics of the therapist can also be obstacles to the therapeutic dialogue. They involve attitudes toward the client. Consider how we sometimes think of our clients or how we discuss them with other therapists. "That one is a borderline and hell to deal with." "He is schizotypal and all over the place." "Oh God, not another manic with verbal diarrhea." "I don't think I can stand the intensity of another extroverted intuitive." "I can't cope with another depressive like him today." "That passive-dependent person is driving me crazy." I have heard these kinds of remarks made about clients off and on during the years I have been a therapist. I have even made them. This does not mean that as therapists we must be saints in our ability to tolerate our clients, but we must be pragmatic. If the therapist approaches the client with anything less than a profound grasp of his unique and inestimable worth, he is not capable of inclusion, and thus he precludes the occurrence of a therapeutic dialogue.

Therapist's Inability to Focus

In addition to the personal attitude of the therapist, there are other obstacles to the dialogue that stem from the therapist's inability to focus his total and undivided concern upon the client. The therapist may be too preoccupied or fatigued. He must take care to maintain himself in such a way that he is able to focus without reservation or distraction upon the welfare of the client. Anything that detracts from his ability to accomplish this precludes the occurrence of the therapeutic dialogue.

Therapist's Inability to Tolerate Client's Pain

The therapist must also be willing to undergo the exposure to the client's psychic state that comes with inclusion, even when sharing this experience is painful. There are times when the therapist, for whatever reasons, is simply not able to tolerate the pain or discomfort associated with such an endeavor. I am reminded of an instance in which a client was recounting his grief associated with the death of his father. The recent death of my own father made inclusion too painful for me and eliminated the possibility of a therapeutic dialogue. From time to time, such limitations on the part of the therapist must be expected.

Therapist's Loss of Personal Awareness

On still other occasions, the therapist may lose his awareness of himself as a person in his empathy with the client and be unable to maintain the dialogue. I experienced such a dilemma with a client who presented himself in my office after two or three weeks of drinking. He was an alcoholic whom I had worked with before. He had been sober for about six months and had recently been able to reestablish his relationship with his wife and his three sons. As I turned, faced him, and looked into his eyes, I felt his misery with such an impact that I totally lost my composure and began to weep. It was impossible for me to stop. I was embarrassed and apologized to the client. I was unable to recover for the remainder of the session. Such is the danger of inclusion if the therapist loses awareness of himself as a person separate and different from the client.

Client's Fear of Close Contact

Just as there can be barriers on the therapist's side, the client may also obstruct the dialogue. The client's total, direct, and open response to the therapist's inclusion is necessary for a therapeutic dialogue to occur. Whatever inhibitions or limitations exist in the client that prevent such a response become obstacles to the therapeutic dialogue. The obstacles result from the client's inability to accommodate the close psychic contact of the therapist's inclusion and to accept the trustworthiness and authenticity of the therapist's concern.

The client may be frightened by the close contact resulting from the therapist's inclusion. He may have had very little experience in dealing with this kind of intimacy with another. It may be an aspect of his existence that he has seldom encountered. Because it is unfamiliar to him, he has no ready response to it. It may be a type of contact that makes him feel extremely vulnerable since there are no barriers, no defenses between him and the therapist's concern. To place himself in such jeopardy may be more than he can tolerate. It is not a matter of trusting the therapist as much as it is of trusting himself to be able to cope with such close psychic contact. We often see our client move away from the close contact of inclusion. There is that moment when contact is being made and you watch the uneasiness of the client. It may be seen in his frightened countenance, his tensed muscles, or changes in his speech. Regardless of how it is expressed, the therapist knows with certainty that the client has eluded contact and aborted the possibility of the dialogue.

Client's Objectivity

Often the client is not open to the dialogue because of his inability to trust the therapist because of his history but also because of the therapist. His interactions with the therapist are guarded. He sets aside a part of himself to watch and protect the rest of him from harm as he responds. This precludes his ability to respond to the therapist's inclusion with all of himself in an open and direct manner. I experienced this phenomenon in the wife of a client. She appeared in my office to express her concerns for her husband. I greeted her in the usual manner, but, in the process of doing so, I complimented her on the beautiful dress she was wearing. Throughout the course of the initial session, she seemed distant and appeared distracted. I felt unable to make contact with her. Finally, approximately ten minutes into the session, she stopped talking to me and had the following conversation with herself without regard for my presence. "I think to myself, what does he want from me? What was he trying to do when he talked about my pretty dress? I wonder if he just wanted to make me feel good. I think, why would he want to do that? Then I think, oh, he just thinks my dress is pretty and that's all there is to it." She then turned her full attention to me for the rest of the session. It had been a personal business that she needed to take care of before she could assume I was trustworthy. The therapist rarely, if ever, encounters such an open and explicit example of the client's struggle with the trust issue. However, in many clients there is a constant internal struggle over trust, making direct contact with the therapist's inclusion impossible.

Client's Distrust of Therapist

In other instances, the client may question the therapist's concern. He may think, "Why would she be concerned for me? After all, it is her job to make me think she is concerned. That's what she is supposed to do, but I don't believe her concern is really authentic." Some time ago, I received a call from a supervisor at a local business asking if I would see one of their employees who was having difficulties. I agreed and soon found myself facing a young woman in her early twenties. I assumed my concern for her had already been established since I had arranged to see her right away. However, I soon found to my surprise that this was not an established fact with the young lady seated before me. She immediately began to question my concern for her. She stated that she could not see how someone like me could help. The only reason I was seeing her was because I was being paid by her employer and not because of my concern for her. We were unable to begin until she was satisfied with the sincerity of my concern.

Summation and Preview

In the first part of this chapter I examined barriers that the therapist might present to a meaningful dialogue. If he approaches the encounter with too much objectivity, he cannot focus his whole being on the client. If he stereotypes his client, he may be unable to concentrate on his wholeness, seeing only his diagnosed disorder. If he is tired or preoccupied, he may lose his focus. At times, he may be unable to endure a client's psychic pain or may become so overwhelmed by it as to lose his effectiveness. All these can be barriers the therapist brings to the encounter, blocking the dialogue.

In examining obstacles to the therapeutic dialogue that may come from the client's side of the interaction, I have not attempted to trace their specific source or raison d'etre. This lies in the client's unique existential history and cannot be found in the analytical work of the therapist nor the introspection of the client.

To analyze the resistance of the client to the therapist's inclusion, one must deal with the client as an object. In such an endeavor (I-It relating), the therapist may be able to formulate a very plausible explanation for the client's resistance. The explanation usually assumes that the cause may be traced to earlier events in the client's life and involves focusing on an event in the client's past that is assumed to have precipitated the resistance to inclusion.

The focus is on some part of the client that must be fixed and not on the whole person. Usually, the more remote the event, the more profound the understanding. The explanation that stems from the analysis generates the feeling in the therapist that he truly understands the client. However, this understanding is entirely different from understanding in the dialogical sense and does nothing to alleviate the resistance in the client. To understand in the dialogical sense is for the therapist to experience the client's resistance as though it were his own.

On the other hand, the client has only introspection to help him understand the source of his resistance, but introspection is limited to his awareness of his inner psychic and physical activities and cannot move beyond them to the ground of his being, his whole self. What does effect understanding and alleviation of his resistance is the meeting with the therapist in the between, something neither the therapist nor the client alone can attain. The source of the client's resistance can be explored meaningfully only in the therapeutic dialogue that the therapist must hope will occur.

To reach the dialogue and the healing between, there must be a beginning. The next chapter examines the initial contact and treatment goals.

15

Initial Client Contact
and Treatment Goals

For the sake of clarity, the dialogical elements and the clinical illustrations thus far have been presented without consideration of the traditional clinical structure within which we as therapists are often required to operate. In this chapter I will attempt to address the concerns of initial client contact and treatment goals as they impinge on the practice of dialogical psychotherapy.

Purpose of Initial Contact

The initial contact involves giving the client an opportunity to experience the therapist in dialogue. That is, the therapist must, in her contact with the client, be open to sharing herself. Such openness is necessary if the client is to relate to her in the close manner required for dialogue. She must be present in a way that produces trust in the client and generates a mutual willingness in both to be undefended in the presence of each other. This requires that she express a genuine concern for the client. To the extent that there is genuine contact, trust, and concern there is the possibility of working with the client in the healing between. This type of intimate, bona fide involvement with the client may not be comfortable for some therapists, but it is a requirement for the practice of dialogical psychotherapy.

The therapist must be open to the client's touchstones. She must be attuned to the unique experiences the client brings to the therapy sessions and respond in a manner that takes into consideration age appropriateness, gender, family, culture, and education of the client. Rapport is best established by presenting ourselves to the client in the same manner we wish to experience him. In this respect the dialogical approach is no different from other approaches.

The dialogical psychotherapist is aware that there is always more to the client than she is encountering at the moment. There are manifold possibilities of being hovering in the shadows of the client's personal wholeness waiting to be accessed. She knows that they are not accessible to the client in his private contemplation and can be actualized only in the encounter that calls them out. Through her imagination she seeks to create the conditions in therapy that can bring about such an encounter. To succeed, she must be attuned to the mystery of the client's existence, always seeking to explore with him those parts of himself that have remained hidden to him in his solitude. She is always prepared for surprises.

Diagnosis in Dialogical Therapy

Traditionally we are trained in our initial contact with the client to seek a diagnosis. This involves identifying patterns of behavior, those characteristics or traits common to a particular disorder that we perceive as persisting in the client. Presumably, this is important since we assume that our client will benefit from the type of treatment given to others who have presented similar symptoms. In many instances this is true if we are content to treat the symptoms and not the whole client.

In our diagnosis we attempt to eliminate surprises. In our desire to understand the client we enter into an analytical process that is structured to eliminate as much as possible the unexpected. Yet the dialogical psychotherapist holds that our most significant encounters with the client's existence may occur in the unexpected—those instances in which the client's uniqueness is expressed. It is in our sharing such a moment with the client that he is able to apprehend what had previously been inaccessible to him and actualize his potential for growth. In our meeting with the unexpected he is able to move beyond the sameness seen in his patterns of behaving that our diagnosis has projected on him.

A young man in his twenties, who was struggling with a career move, illustrates what can happen when we become attuned to the uniqueness of our experiences. George had been wrestling for weeks with a job change. He was stuck in his ruminations of what might happen if he made a move. As the session began, I asked him what had happened since the last time I had seen him. He replied, "Oh, nothing but the same old thing. I'm still worried about changing jobs and can't seem to make up my mind." I gently informed him that this could not be. There was no way that the same thing could be happening over and over. Something different was happening each time he entered into his struggle with a job change. If nothing else, he had never struggled with it at that time in that place. I asked him to give some thought to what there was about his struggle the previous week that was different from his prior struggles. He thought for a moment and stated that last week when he talked with his wife about the problem, she agreed that he ought to consider changing jobs. She had never before offered him such support. At that moment, when he remembered her support he became animated and began to talk with positive enthusiasm about his job change. He became so positive that within a week he had committed himself to a new job offer. Up to this point he had focused on the sameness of his experiences to the exclusion of their uniqueness in which his growth occurred.

Dialogically speaking, the diagnosis is important because it identifies the manifestations of the client's disturbance and gives us a way of communicating with one another about the client—talking about the client as opposed to talking to the client. But it can be a means of focusing the attention of the therapist on the repetitions or sameness in the client's experiences to the exclusion of his uniqueness. Although the client's expression of the diagnosis may appear to be similar to others, his experiences of it are always unique. It is in his personal experience of the diagnosis that the real work of therapy occurs. The dialogical psychotherapist recognizes the importance of diagnosis but is careful to remember that a diagnostic label never encompasses the unique wholeness of the client. This is seen in the attempts of the therapist to work in the elusive area of the client's uniqueness which by its very nature is always a mystery. It can be anticipated but it cannot be preconceived. It can be experienced, but it cannot be defined. It is, by its very nature, always a surprise.

Treatment Goals

The treatment goals of the traditional clinical approach address the identified psychopathology of the client—those psychic or mental activities that we presume have produced his disturbance. The traditional therapist assumes that the meaning of the symptom is found in its psychological causes. The treatment goals are structured to alleviate the cause and thus remove the client's disturbance. The therapist believes that to accomplish the task requires formulating clear and concise goals based on the psychological diagnosis. The effectiveness of the therapeutic process is seen in the client's movement toward the fulfillment of these goals. The extent of the client's movement is measured by the accomplishment of certain explicitly stated treatment objectives that are commensurate with the goals. Since the objectives address the client's intrapsychic activities, it is not an easy task to state them in a manner that makes them publicly observable. Verification is usually accomplished by noting the client's verbal reports and/or his behavior in the clinical setting, which are assumed to be reliable and valid indicators of intrapsychic changes.

The dialogical psychotherapist contends that we cannot treat the whole client if we assume the meaning of the client's symptom is found solely in its psychological cause. We must also be concerned with its purpose, that is, what the symptom is intended to accomplish in the client's existence. We can see this in existential guilt in which the origin of the symptom is found in the client's injury of a relationship. We speak of this event as the cause of the symptom. Yet, alleviating the symptom—feeling guilty—does not remove the guilt, which is ontic or actual. The symptom has a

purpose to accomplish in the client's existence and remains with
him until he has gone through the threefold process necessary for
reconciliation: illumination, acceptance, and reconciliation.

In the case of neurotic guilt, there is no ontic guilt, only guilt
feelings, but these feelings also have a purpose. Although their
cause is found in the injured relationship, the injury is the result
of others (family and/or society) who have imposed their demands
on the client without regard for what he is uniquely intended to be.
The client is usually concerned with alleviation of the symptoms.
The purpose of the symptoms, however, is to help him reclaim his
wholeness, severed because of the injury he has suffered.

Case Examples

A clinical example comes to mind in which the client was damaged
by the mistreatment she suffered from her parents. Connie was a
fifty-year-old widow. Her husband had died several years prior to
her seeing me. She came to see me because of her anguish at being
left alone and helpless in the world. The turning point came in the
third session. As she sat on the couch before me she began writhing
in pain, screaming out in anger at her dead parents. "Why! Why!
did you raise me to be so helpless. It's not fair." As she rocked back
and forth like an autistic child, I asked her to hold her misery close
and let it do the work it needed to do in her. She screamed out, "All
it does is make me more and more angry at my parents and my
husband for leaving me in such a helpless state. Why did they do
that to me?" I replied as kindly as I could, "Hold your misery to
you again for it has not done its work with you yet. It will visit you
again and again until it has accomplished its purpose." The session
ended with Connie still feeling hurt and sorry for herself.

In the next session, Connie was very subdued. I asked her
once again to hold her misery close to her and see where it took her.
I watched as she struggled to comply. In the next few moments, I
began to see a distinct change in her. Toward the end of the session
she stated that she was beginning to see what I meant when I said
the misery had something it wanted to do with her. It was to get
her to take control of her life.

Slowly across the following sessions I began to see Connie

take control of her life. She enrolled in a training course, obtained her real estate license, and began selling homes. Several years later she returned to school and became a social worker. She has since called me on several occasions to share her accomplishments with me. In spite of my protestations, she still feels that I was the one who saved her life. It was not I but her symptom, her misery, that did the work.

I recently saw a patient who exemplifies the tendency in some clients to seek alleviation of their symptoms without concern for their purpose, that is, what they were intended to accomplish in their lives. Ed was in his forties, in good health, and in the midst of a severe crisis. He had been an executive in a large firm that sold automobiles. He had worked hard to arrive at his position in his corporation. His salary had been well into the six figure range. He had owned a large home in a very prestigious neighborhood, had been happily married, and had a nine-year-old son whom he loved very much.

Ed came to see me because his world had crumbled around him. His corporation had begun losing money and he had been relieved of his position. His wife had left him for another man and had taken his son with her. He was mentally and emotionally devastated. He stated that what he really needed was to rid himself of his depression and anxiety. He just wanted to feel better. He asked that I refer him to a psychiatrist who could prescribe medication for his anxiety and depression. He was set on alleviating his symptoms.

Ed was not concerned about the purpose of his symptoms. He just wanted to be rid of them. It never occurred to him that they might have a purpose to perform in his life. To him, they were no more than the results of what had happened to him. When I attempted to discuss their purpose in his life, he was perplexed. He countered that if he was to do anything about his situation he must first get rid of the feelings he was having. He indicated that what he really wanted was to stop the direction in which his life was going and return to where he had been before all this had happened. Since this was impossible, he at least wanted to feel better. He was not concerned with the work he needed to do to feel better; the medication would take care of it. The only help Ed wanted from me was a referral so he could secure medication.

Ontically speaking, the meaning of the symptom unfolds in the dialogue. Since there was no dialogue with Ed, we can only speculate about the purpose of his symptoms. Certainly his depression was appropriate in view of his loss of job and family. His anxiety was normal for one who faced such uncertainty. We can reason that the depression was necessary to effect the mourning process required for Ed to accept his losses and reorganize his existence. We can assume that the arousal generated by his anxiety was necessary to alert him to the possibilities that were presented to him in his attempts to deal with his new concerns.

However, the purpose of the symptoms is unique to Ed. It is in his interaction with the therapist that their purpose emerges. The outcome is a mystery and cannot be anticipated since it is peculiar to the dialogue. This uncertainty has profound implications for the dialogical psychotherapist. She must always be aware that she can only experience the purpose of the client's symptoms in her interaction with his wholeness, a personal wholeness that can only be encountered in dialogue and that cannot be encompassed in the treatment goals.

This approach does not mean the dialogical therapist is opposed to formulating treatment goals for they provide direction and substance to the therapeutic dialogue. However, she does not believe a satisfactory resolution of the client's disturbance can be found solely in its psychological causes. It is her contention that the client and the therapist must be willing to move beyond psychological concerns to the ontological—the client's pursuit of his personal direction—for complete resolution.

Summation and Preview

The dialogical approach requires concern for the personal direction of the client; this concern is seen in the therapist's interest in the nature of the client's movement in therapy, a movement that involves the wholeness of the client. In traditional treatment, goals are formulated to promote movement toward the alleviation of specific distresses that arise from conflicts in the client's psyche. They are not designed for the ontological concerns of the client, the client's pursuit of his personal direction. Since the nature of the client's movement in such a pursuit unfolds in the dialogue, it cannot be formulated in treatment goals designed to focus on conflicts between specific aspects of the client's being—his psychopathology. Such treatment goals are designed to be accomplished by analyzing the client. The dialogical approach attempts to synthesize the client. It is concerned with the unique wholeness of the client, which is inaccessible apart from dialogue. As the client's unique wholeness unfolds in the dialogue, the personal direction of the client emerges. It is a movement toward the fulfillment of what the client is intended to be. The next chapter examines the unfolding of the treatment process.

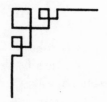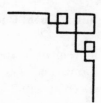

16

The Unfolding
of the Treatment Process

From the dialogical perspective, the unfolding of the treatment process is a mystery that cannot be anticipated nor encompassed in the treatment goals. The dynamic of the healing process is found in a reality beyond both the therapist and the client and is under the control of neither. Since the healing occurs between them in their interaction, it cannot be planned or developed. Healing can only be apprehended as it unfolds in the dialogue, which comes by grace. The dialogical psychotherapist must be willing to accommodate the unpredictable and uncertain nature of the dialogical process. While it is true that the diagnosis provides a starting point and treatment goals give a direction to the therapeutic process, once we have encountered the uniqueness of the client our journey has only one destination: wherever the mystery of the between leads us.

Case Example: Regaining Wholeness

Sam was married and had four young children. He worked for a large company and was doing well, financially. He had come to see me because of his difficulty with the police due to exposing himself. He was very anxious and depressed and I gave him two diagnoses based on diagnostic categories of the American Psychiatric Association (1987): adjustment disorder with mixed emotional features (DSM-III-R 309.28) and exhibitionism (DSM-III-R 302.40).

The treatment goals consisted of alleviating Sam's anxiety and depression and assisting him in regaining control of his exhibitionism. Some of the treatment objectives were to reduce his tension so that he could function on the job, assist him to sleep without interruption, remove his sense of hopelessness, and assist him to function without reverting to unacceptable episodes of exhibitionism.

As the treatment sessions progressed, Sam revealed what he thought was the origin of his exhibitionism. As he was entering puberty he discovered that if he positioned himself just right while undressing in the school gymnasium he could be seen by the girls in their dressing room. Several of the girls seemed to delight in his exposure of himself. This went on throughout the school year, giving Sam much pleasure. He felt it was at this time that he learned to exhibit himself to females. He reported that much to his liking the girls seemed to want to watch him more than they wanted to expose themselves to him. Since that time he had sought opportunities to expose himself.

Sam reported that in the course of his exhibitionism he had learned to separate his sexual expressions from his loving. He had found it very comforting to allow women to admire his penis as an alternative to penile-vaginal sex. When he could not find willing subjects, he went to massage parlors and paid women to view him. He spoke with great delight of how exciting it was to have a woman whom he did not know look at his penis. He reported that it was a wonderful way to experience sexual feelings without intimacy.

Although Sam did not feel his life-style had adversely affected his relationship with his wife, it had limited the manner in which he could have sex with her. He could have sex with her only if it did not involve intimate emotional contact. He protested that he loved his wife but had to keep his sex with her separate from his love for her. He had no problems hugging and kissing her, but this was loving and never sexual. The moment it became sexual, it was unacceptable to him. He felt his wife had learned to accept his peculiarities, although as far as he knew, she was not aware of all of his exhibitionistic adventures outside the home. From time to time during these discussions, I sensed Sam's aloneness and commented on how difficult it must be for him to maintain such aloofness in his sexual expressions. His response was always to avoid acknowledging such feelings.

Sam and I both agreed that the inappropriate expression of his exhibitionism had always occurred when he had been drinking excessively. He developed a drinking pattern that precluded his drinking excessively while not at home. He reduced his drinking outside his home to no more than two beers. During the ensuing weeks, he reported his ability to maintain this pattern of drinking. He found this very satisfactory and felt he had at last gained control of his exhibitionism. His case with the police was about to be settled, and I began to prepare for termination of our sessions.

I reviewed our treatment contract and reminded Sam that we had accomplished what he had wanted. He had indicated that he was feeling good about himself again and that he felt everything was under control. As I went through the motions of termination, I felt deeply disappointed that I had shared so little of what Sam could be. He was so much more than a penis he loved to display. What he had told me led me to believe that his exhibitionism was ego-syntonic and he did not see any reason to change. He only wanted to control it.

Much to my surprise, as the final session was closing, Sam shifted uneasily on the couch and said, "I want to stop this business of sex without intimacy. I want to love my wife only. Help me to find a way to be with her and only love and have sex with her. I don't like the way I am." I was deeply touched by his request. In that moment Sam had redefined our treatment contract. The treatment goals that had resulted from the diagnosis had been completed. The part of Sam that had been psychologically diagnosed had been fixed, but his wholeness was still fragmented and divided, leaving him disturbed. The therapy had dealt with the causes of his symptoms, but it had not addressed their purpose. It is in Sam's pursuit of the purpose of his symptoms that he will apprehend his personal direction and unify his fragmented self. It is my hope that this will occur as Sam's treatment process continues to unfold.

Dialogically speaking, the meaning of our life is found in the fulfillment of our purpose. Our purpose is found in the expression of our uniqueness. Our uniqueness can be expressed only by our whole self in response to a concrete event. The nature of this response is seen in our I–Thou relationships. To the extent that we respond to each concrete event with our unified wholeness there is purpose and meaning in our life and we experience a personal direction. This was certainly not so in the case of Sam. His disturbance was the product of his aborted interactions with others. His exhibitionistic encounters with females were never with his unified wholeness. He always interacted with less than his whole self. His life was not moving in a meaningful direction. He was stuck in a repetitive way of being that he found unfulfilling. There was no personal direction in his life.

The personal direction of our lives unfolds in those moments when we respond with our whole being to a concrete event that calls forth our potential. It appears in that moment when there is an interface of the ontological and the psychological facets of our existence—in our response to the event—and is not accessible to us before the event calls it out. The response cannot be anticipated and there is no event before it to which it can be traced. We only know in that moment that it is the right response for us, right in the sense that it is the only response appropriate in that situation. It originates in the very ground of our being and moves our existence in a personal direction that is uniquely ours. From the dialogical perspective, there is no way we or any other can know before the event what we are intended to be. It constantly unfolds as we bring our whole being to the encounter.

Case Example: Finding Personal Direction

An example is Joseph, who came for treatment of his substance abuse. Subsequent to his detoxification, he had sought the help of a psychiatrist who had prescribed medication for his anxiety and depression. He stated that he did not want to take the medication, but he was frightened not to for at least six months until he had sufficiently recovered from his prolonged use of drugs. Yet, he knew it was dangerous to take drugs to get off drugs. His friends all felt this was contrary to living a drug-free life. He struggled with the problem throughout the session and asked me to tell him what to do. I suggested that he see where his feelings took him. This would mean staying with his feelings until they had accomplished their purpose. He stated that he did not understand what I meant, but he would try. I replied that he felt he knew the cause of his feelings, but he had not focused on what they were trying to accomplish in his life. He seemed perplexed, but agreed to make an effort.

The following week Joseph opened the session by explaining what had happened to him in response to my suggestion of the previous session. He said:

> I left the last session feeling bad, but I decided to try and go along with my feelings and see where they took me. The first thing I did was to lose my appointment book, and I did not know when I was supposed to see the psychiatrist to get the medication. I called his office and got the time I was supposed to see him. I hung up and within a few minutes I had once again forgotten it. I called his office again and asked. His secretary was now a little irritated with me. I was careful to write it down on a piece of paper so I would not forget. A little later I found I had lost the paper. I started to call again, when I realized I did not want to see a psychiatrist to take a drug to stop taking drugs. I then called his office and told his secretary I did not want to see him. Instead of just trying to get rid of my feelings I went along with them to see where they would take me.

In his struggle Joseph had found his personal direction in that situation.

Case Example: Meeting Problem with Wholeness

Another example is Cynthia, a married woman in her late sixties. Her primary problem was the twenty-eight-year-old daughter of her husband from a previous marriage: the daughter wanted to move in and live with them. She described the daughter as a person who was over six feet tall and weighed well over two hundred pounds. Cynthia felt extremely intimidated by her. Previously, I had helped her select a new career for herself and was struck by her amiability. She was a pleasant woman who was very loving and caring of those around her. She had recently married for the second time and was deeply in love. She stated that her present husband had brought meaning back into her life and she could not think of living without him. Yet if she said no to having his daughter live with them, she was sure he would leave her. I stood with her as she struggled with her dilemma. At one point in the session, she grabbed my hand and wept as she cried out in her anguish, "I don't know what to do. I must say no for I cannot live with the intimidation, yet if I say no, I'm sure my husband will leave me. Oh, Doctor Heard, I'm going to lose him. How will I live without him? Yet, I cannot live with the fear of his daughter." At this point, she fell back on the couch and sobbed. I responded by telling her that she had within her what she needed to cope with the situation and it would be there when she faced her husband. She continued to sob as she spoke, "I don't feel it. I don't know what to do." She left the session expressing doubt about her ability to cope with the situation.

Out of concern, I asked Cynthia to call me after she had faced her husband and let me know how she was doing. She called later and stated everything was fine and she would see me on Monday of the coming week. I thought, as calm as she was, she had in all probability not confronted her husband but had acquiesced as was usual for her and did not want to discuss it with me.

On the following Monday she appeared in my office highly animated. She reported, "Doctor Heard, it was the darndest thing. I was literally scared to death when I sat down at the kitchen table to discuss the matter with my husband. I did not know what I was going to do until I started to talk. The moment I started talking I knew exactly what I had to say. I told my husband how I felt and that even if it meant losing him I could not do what he was asking me to do." She went on to explain, "We sat and talked for three hours about our relationship. We were drawn closer to each other than we have ever been. Not only were we closer, but I took his daughter out for dinner and told her of my feelings. It was a wonderful experience for both of us. She was able to connect my feelings about her to her experiences with her boy friends. She said I had been very helpful to her. She agreed that the decision was a good one and she would move in with her friends who wanted her. As it ended up, we were all drawn closer together. I cannot tell you how happy I am that I faced my fear and confronted the issue with my husband." Throughout the session she frequently expressed her astonishment over her ability to speak out. She said, "I don't know where it came from. You told me it was in me. Why could I not see it?"

Danger of Fragmentation

The dialogical psychotherapist attempts to relate to the client in a manner that encompasses his manifold possibilities of being. There is a particularity in such relationships that is not present in our other interactions. When we interact with nature, a creature of nature, or a work of art, we bring whatever we choose of our possibilities for relating to the event. However, the other in such cases has only one way of relating to us, with whatever it is—the wholeness of its being. It is not possible for the other in such cases to withhold a part of itself from the interaction. Such withholding seems to be exclusively limited to human beings.

Our relations with humans is distinctively different. As humans, we have the ability to choose what we will bring to the relationship. We may choose to interact with the other as an object who possesses certain characteristics or functions, or we may choose to interact with the other's unique wholeness. When both of us bring our wholeness to the interaction there is the possibility of a dialogue.

The differences of the partners in a relationship such as age, familial status, gender, ethnic origin, religion, and social structure present the possibility of one having an advantage over the other. For example, a child soon learns that he cannot relate to his parents in his wholeness unless he is encouraged to do so. The effect of such a relationship was seen in the case of Alex whose parents related to him as a child who was inadequate and undeserving of love (see Chapter Seven).

Regardless of the reasons, when the other chooses not to interact with our wholeness, there is a danger of our being impaired. When this occurs we are fragmented. Our possibilities of being, which have been denied recognition in the relationship, are severed from our unified wholeness and become inaccessible to us (unconscious). This can be seen in the case of Sam, when he felt the young females related to him as a sex object to be viewed. His possibility of being more than this in his intimate interactions with other females was severed from his unified wholeness. If there is to be restoration of his unified wholeness, the severed possibility must be reclaimed and confirmed in dialogue with the therapist. Restoration of Cynthia's wholeness was seen in her assertion after the inclusion and confirmation she received in our dialogue.

Impairments from I-It Relationships

Most of the impairments I have seen in clients seem to have occurred in I-It relationships, that is, when the client has been consistently related to as an object. The client has been coerced into conforming to the wishes of the other and has assumed that this was appropriate for him without any consideration of his own uniqueness. He has lost touch with his wholeness in his attempt to comply with the demands of others and has assumed that is the way he is in the world.

An example is Claude, who appeared in my office complaining of obsessive-compulsive behavior. He stated that it had gotten so bad that he could no longer function. It had impaired his relationships and was affecting his work performance. He worried constantly and found it impossible to make a decision for fear of making a mistake. He had been on medication to control it, but the medicine did not seem to help. He spoke of his obsessive-compulsive behavior as if it did not belong to him, and he was under its control. I could feel his sense of helplessness as he struggled to gain control of his life. He pleaded with me to help him.

Case Example: Danger of Adopting Another's Touchstones

As the treatment process unfolded, Claude recounted how as a child he had been called on to help with the younger siblings in the absence of the father. His mother had been injured in an accident and was bedridden. His body shook as he sobbed while speaking of how sorry he was for his mother. He talked of how difficult it was for him to perform chores around the household for her. It became increasingly obvious as the session progressed that Claude had been impaired in his interactions with his mother. She had, whether intending to or not, imposed her expectations on Claude in her interactions with him. He had responded as if he were meant to be her helper. His function had been to make certain her tasks were correctly performed and on time, and he was to make no mistakes. One could see how in his interactions with his mother he had acquired his obsessive-compulsive traits.

These traits had been useful to Claude in certain areas of his life as he was growing up. He found, as a student, he could stay at his studies much longer than the other students. But now as he had entered another phase in his life, the traits no longer served him well. He had never married, although he had a good job. However, his need always to be right—to keep at the task until he was certain it was right—was a problem. He could not overcome his fear of not being right no matter how hard he tried. In his attempts to do so, he repeatedly went over the task in his mind. Often he performed the same task over and over, even though he had done it right the first time, in his attempts to be certain he was right. His efforts were never sufficient to give him the assurance he needed.

For most of Claude's life he had felt that this was just the way he was, but lately it had become such a burden to him that he could no longer stand it. It was when he sought to rid himself of the traits that he began to experience them as if they did not belong to him. In a sense this was true; they belonged to his mother who had imposed them on him. The task in therapy was to assist Claude in the dialogue to reclaim his unique wholeness, which had been fragmented in his childhood interactions with his mother.

Claude's task was further confounded by the fact that such traits are necessary if he is to function successfully in the world. It was his inability to moderate their use in his life—to determine how much concern is appropriate in each situation—that was the problem. I am speaking of the appropriate interplay of I-Thou and I-It relations in Claude's life. It would be naive to assume that Claude can maintain such a balance without great difficulty when it is in conflict with the way he has learned to function in the world. For this reason, as the treatment process unfolded, Claude had to decide whether he would continue to tolerate the misery of his fragmentation or subject himself to the fear and uncertainty of assuming a life stance that was commensurate with his dialogical touchstones. The empowerment of his decision to pursue his personal direction will unfold in the mystery of the between, which we hope is present in the therapeutic process.

The Mystery of Healing

Some therapeutic approaches assume a knowledge of the therapeutic process that removes this mystery. The process is no more than the application of techniques that have evolved from certain theoretical and empirical considerations. A description of the process focuses on those characteristics and traits of the client that will be influenced by the therapist's skillful application of the appropriate techniques. The explicitness of the description enhances the empirical validation of the approach and is assumed to be a measure of its theoretical efficacy. In summary, some clinical approaches assume the client needs something and the therapeutic process is designed to accomplish it. These approaches also assume that they can describe what this something is and how it is to be accomplished. Several clinical approaches do not hesitate to apply the scientific method. In other words, it is possible to have a science of therapeutic process. This way of thinking is contrary to the dialogical approach.

If a description of the therapy process involves explaining how the healing of the client's disturbed self is accomplished in the therapeutic endeavor, the dialogical psychotherapist will be found wanting. He or she holds that this type of therapy is not amenable to analysis utilizing the methodology of natural science. From the dialogical perspective there are at least three characteristics of the therapy process that make such a scientific analysis impossible. First, the healing process is not observable; second, it is unique; and third, the dynamic of the between is not subject to a natural order.

Healing Is Not Publicly Observable

It may be argued that the first of these objections, the lack of being observable, can be overcome by the use of intervening variables in our theoretical constructs. This is a common practice in our clinical endeavors. We assume the client's behavior, including his verbal reports, are valid indicators of his intrapsychic activities that cannot be directly observed.

Healing Is Unique

The second characteristic, uniqueness, is not so easily overcome. How can a unique event be analyzed? There is nothing to which it can be compared since it has no counterpart. Scientific analysis thrives on explicit descriptions, making it possible to sort events into appropriate classifications, noting their similarities and differences, generating frequency counts, and studying how the antecedent and subsequent events are connected. None of this is possible when the event is unique. The uniqueness is seen throughout the therapy process in the participants, both the therapist and the client, and in their interaction.

Healing Is Not Subject to Natural Order

The third characteristic, that the process is not subject to a natural order, is an additional barrier to scientific analysis. The healing dynamic of the dialogical process is found in a third reality, the between, which comes by grace. Its occurrence is not subject to a predictable order for there are no contingencies that guarantee its occurrences nor can its impact on the partners of the interaction be predicted or comprehended. If it occurs, it will be only when each partner brings his wholeness to the relationship; even then, when it does occur, it always comes by grace. The dynamic of the dialogical therapeutic process is not amenable to scientific analysis.

The Work of the Between

It is true that with some therapeutic approaches there is a fixing of sorts that occurs outside of dialogue. However, such fixing is at best applicable only to our ongoing functioning as embodied creatures. The part of our being that can be analyzed is the part that is shared with other animals. This part belongs to a being who is very sophisticated, but still an animal—an animal who is capable of learning from its experiences as well as communicating such acquired knowledge to others of its species, even passing it on to future generations; an animal who can enhance the adjustment skills of itself and others; an animal who can develop procedures (scientific methodology) for studying and manipulating its environment. But the restoration of our wholeness is not found in that part of ourselves that is like other animals but in our humanness, which is found in our dialogue with others as a corollary of the healing between.

From the dialogical perspective, the source of healing is found in the meeting of the client and the therapist. However, in many approaches to therapy, the meeting is assumed to provide only a means whereby certain things can be accomplished in the client that promote his healing. The meeting itself is not the source of healing but rather a context in which the therapist can obtain information about the client's disturbance and apply the appropriate techniques to eliminate it. The emphasis is on the analytical and technical skills of the therapist and not the dialogical process. The contention is that the therapist does something to the client and/or persuades the client to do something to himself in the meeting that alleviates the disturbance.

To the contrary, Friedman tells us, "It [the meeting] is not only the means to the goal; it is itself the goal" (1985, p. 218). Healing comes in the meeting itself and not in the application of the analytical and technical skills of the therapist. The actual source of the healing comes from a reality, the between, that appears in the meeting of the client and the therapist.

Each occurrence of the healing between is unique and beyond our comprehension. It can be apprehended only in what it brings about in our personal wholeness. It is ontically indigenous to us and singularly defines our humanness. It is the eternal Thou which is met in the meeting with our temporal Thou. It does not exist in our understanding but in the meeting. It is encountered in that which emerges between us and the other in our interaction with the other. It is our only entree to the actual existence of the client and is not encountered in our diagnostic and theoretical conjuring that focuses on his psychological traits and/or characteristics. It is in the between that the real therapy process unfolds.

I have on occasions experienced the work of the between in a most startling manner. Recently, while working with a client, the presence of this reality swept over me. In that moment, I felt as if a powerful energizing force had passed through me. I watched as the client's composure was momentarily shaken. He hesitated for a moment then rattled off several things as if he were supposed to respond but did not know how. He then said, "That's what I came to therapy for." The session, for all practical purposes, was over. He had gotten what he wanted and was ready to leave.

On another occasion, a kind of quiet assurance came over me as I spoke to the client. Shortly, the client said, "From time to time as I talk with you something is happening to me. For just an instant every once in awhile I get a glimpse of my whole self. I find it both exciting and frightening." She had come to see me because of un-predictable panic attacks. In the next session she related several significant but positive changes that had occurred the week after the session that she could not understand. She was bewildered. She stated that she no longer felt the panicky need for her lover. She was single and had been involved in a long-standing relationship with a married man. She spoke of her intention not to see him anymore. In relation to her panic, she told how she had intentionally left her purse in her desk drawer while she went outside for a cigarette. On the way back, she felt almost desperate when she realized she needed to go to the restroom before returning to her desk to check on her purse. However, she was able to regain her composure long enough to go to the restroom before returning to her desk. This was the first time in ten years that she had been able to go anywhere without her purse, which contained medication for anxiety. She had never taken the medication in all that time but had always had a supply in her purse just in case she needed it. She felt something had been changed in her, but she did not know how to explain it. She spoke of seeing me for one more session and then terminating since she had gotten what she wanted from the therapy. Apart from the work of the between, I have no way of explaining such happenings. I cannot find a satisfactory explanation in my previous psychological training.

Discomfort to Therapist of Dialogical Approach

For many of us the type of intimate involvement with the client required in the practice of dialogical psychotherapy is too frightening or uncomfortable to engage in. For others, entrusting the client's healing to the between, which cannot be predicted or controlled, is too incompatible with our training to be embraced. Some of us see this type of therapy as irrational. We cannot tolerate the mystery of the between. Yet, we must surrender ourselves to the work of the between if we wish to help the whole client. We must bring our wholeness to our interactions with the client. As therapists, we cannot relate to the wholeness of the client without bringing our own wholeness to the interactions. For most of us, this is a very threatening experience. However, it is impossible for us to practice dialogical psychotherapy without experiencing significant changes in our own lives.

Personally, there have been significant changes in my life since embracing the dialogical approach. My attitude toward my clients has been compellingly altered. I have learned that the dialogical process does not lend itself to anything less than my total participation. For whatever reason, if I am distracted or not present with the client, the healing between is not present. It has required that I approach each client as a person of inestimable value with his own unique personal direction that must unfold in the dialogue. I have learned that the dialogical process does not lend itself to manipulation. The approach has demanded that I give up any notions I might hold regarding my personal ability to heal the disturbed client. Although I may approach the client armed with certain skills and techniques derived from a particular theoretical orientation, these are useless unless the healing between is present. At best, they are expressions of my concern for the client and do not have the power to heal. I have learned that those who are called healers have always been dialogical regardless of their awareness of the process. Our ability to identify or attempt to articulate the dialogical process has nothing to do with its effectiveness when it is practiced.

Looking Ahead

As we consider explicating dialogical psychotherapy, it is essential that we focus on the dialogue for it unfolds in the sphere of the between, which is the dynamic of the therapy process. Distancing and relating as well as inclusion and confirmation in early childhood with their implications for developmental psychology have yet to be defined. The therapeutic effects of inclusion as it relates to transference and countertransference are in need of explication. The richness of the unconscious awaits exploration. No one has yet fully explored the dialogical as it relates to psychotherapy. Other areas such as developmental psychology, the etiology of psychopathology, and personality theory from the dialogical perspective have yet to be delineated.

This introduction to dialogical psychotherapy is not intended to be a definitive work. It is at best evocative, as I hope that my colleagues will join the endeavor even as others have preceded it. The dialogical is rich in possibilities. It offers a working perspective for the interface of the ontological and psychological facets of our existence, the reality of the between, which is beyond psychology. It is in the mystery of the between, not in ourselves, that we acquire our humanness and the real work of healing originates.

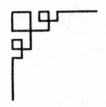
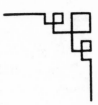

References
and
Suggested Readings

American Psychiatric Association. *Diagnostic and Statistical Manual of Mental Disorders.* (3rd ed., rev.). Washington, D.C.: American Psychiatric Association, 1987.

Barrett, W. *Irrational Man.* New York: Doubleday, 1958.

Boszormenyi-Nagy, I., and Krasner, B. R. *Between Give and Take: A Clinical Guide to Contextual Therapy.* New York: Brunner/Mazel, 1986.

Boszormenyi-Nagy, I., and Spark, G. *Invisible Loyalties: Reciprocity in Intergenerational Family Therapy.* New York: HarperCollins, 1973.

Buber, M. *Eclipse of God.* New York: HarperCollins, 1952.

Buber, M. *Pointing the Way: Selected Essays.* (M. S. Friedman, trans. and ed.) Atlantic Highlands, N.J.: Humanities Press, 1957.

Buber, M. *I and Thou.* (R. G. Smith, trans.) (2nd ed. rev.) New York: Charles Scribner's Sons, 1958.

Buber, M. *The Origin and Meaning of Hasidism.* (M. S. Friedman, trans. and ed.) New York: Horizon Books, 1960.

Buber, M. *Daniel: Dialogues on Realization.* (M. S. Friedman, trans. and ed.) Troy, MO: Holt, Rinehart & Winston, 1965a.

Buber, M. *Between Man and Man*. (R. G. Smith, trans.) New York: Macmillan, 1965b.

Buber, M. *A Believing Humanism: My Testament, 1902-1965*. (M. S. Friedman, trans. and ed.) Atlantic Highlands, N.J.: Humanities Press, 1967.

Buber, M. *The Knowledge of Man: Selected Essays*. (M. S. Friedman and R. G. Smith, trans.) Atlantic Highlands, N.J.: Humanities Press, 1988.

Farber, L. H. *The Ways of the Will. Essays Toward a Psychology and Psychopathology of the Will*. New York: Basic Books, 1966.

Farber, L. H. *Lying, Despair, Jealousy, Envy, Sex, Suicide, Drugs, and the Good Life*. New York: Basic Books, 1967.

Friedman, A. M. *Treating Chronic Pain: The Healing Partnership*. New York: Plenum, 1992.

Friedman, M. S. *Martin Buber: The Life of Dialogue*. (3rd ed. rev.) Chicago: University of Chicago Press, 1960.

Friedman, M. S. *Touchstones of Reality: Existential Trust and the Community of Peace*. New York: Dutton, 1972.

Friedman, M. S. *The Healing Dialogue in Psychotherapy*. New York: Jason Aronson, 1985.

Friedman, M. S. (ed.). *The Worlds of Existentialism: A Critical Reader*. Atlantic Highlands, N.J.: Humanities Press, 1991.

Friedman, M. S. *Dialogue and the Human Image: Beyond Humanistic Psychology*. Newburg Park, Calif.: Sage, 1992a.

Friedman, M. S. *Religion and Psychology: A Dialogical Approach*. New York: Paragon House, 1992b.

Hycner, R. H. *Between Person and Person: Toward a Dialogical Psychotherapy*. Hyland, N.Y.: Center for Gestalt Development, 1991.

Jordan, J. V., Kaplan, A. G., Miller, J. B., Stiver, I. P., and Surrey, J. L. *Women's Growth in Connection: Writings from the Stone Center*. New York: Guilford Press, 1991.

Pascal, B. *Pascal's Pensees*. (H. F. Stewart, trans.) New York: Pantheon Books, 1965. (Originally published 1676.)

Trüb, H. *Heilung aus der Begegnung. Eine Auseinandersetzung mit der Psychologie C. G. Jungs*. (E. Michel and A. Sborowitz, eds.) Stuttgart: Ernst Klett Verlag, 1952.

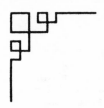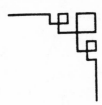

Index

A

Abandonment, fear of, 19

Acceptance: of pain, 84; of wholeness, 80, 81–82

Activity, to avoid uncertainty, 117–118

Addiction: disease model of, 109; recovery from, 108–109, 115, 145–146

Adjustment disorder, 143

Alcoholics, adult children of: and excessive I-It relating, 35–36; healing of, using the between, 18–19; and neurotic guilt, 107

Alienation, source of, 114

American Psychiatric Association, 30, 46, 143

Analysis, limitations of: in accessing unconscious, 62–63, 65; in accessing wholeness, 81, 126; versus benefits of, 128; in finding personal direction, 53; in healing, 151–153; versus synthesis, 43; in understanding clients' resistance, 132–133; in understanding dreams, 71, 72. *See also* Scientific method

Anxiety: alleviating versus finding purpose in, 139, 143, 145–146; in encountering the between, 60; healing of, through dialogue and the unconscious, 65–67, 154; healing of, through touchstone dialogue, 120–121

Apperception: human ability of, 32; and reality, 112; and relating within self, 33–34, 62

Apprehension, versus comprehension, 112

Approval: and confirmation, 97–98; using seeming to obtain, 81, 95

Avoidant personality disorder, therapy for, 45

Awareness: and dialogue, 28; and resolving guilt, 103; and wholeness, 11–12

Index

D

De Leo, J., 58

Defenses: dialogical interpretation of, 63; against feeling inadequate, 64; against pursuit of personal direction, 115–120

Dependency: in childhood, 87; and exploitation, 87–89; and finding personal direction, 116–117; healing of, through actualizing potential wholeness, 61–62; healing of, using the between, 18–19; and inclusion, 88; and thickening the distance, 38

Depression: alleviating versus finding purpose in, 139, 143, 145–146; and avoiding touchstones, 117–118; source of, 45

Desire, versus action, 55

Diagnosis, in dialogical versus traditional psychotherapy, 135–137

Diagnostic and Statistical Manual (DSM-III-R) (American Psychiatric Association), 30. *See also* DSM-III-R diagnostic categories

Dialogical, the, 10, 23. *See also* Dialogue

Dialogical psychotherapy: clinical considerations of, 125–156; diagnosis in, 135–137; discomfort to therapists of, 155–156; elements of, 10–13; future of, 156; goal of, 95; importance of, 7–13; initial contact in, 134–135; nature of, 9–10; and philosophical anthropology, 1, 2–3, 7–8; requirement of intimacy in, 135; versus traditional psychotherapy, 135–156; treatment goals in, 137–138; treatment process in, 142–156. *See also* Between, the; Case examples, in psychotherapy; Confirmation; Dialogical, the; Dialogue; Distancing; Dreams; Existential guilt; Healing; Inclusion; Mutuality; Personal direction; Touchstones; Unconscious, the

Dialogue: barriers to, 114, 127–132; case examples of, 27–30, 31, 120–121; characteristics of, 24–26; confirmation in, 93, 98–100; dreams as incomplete, 68–69, 71–77; exploitation in, 91–92; finding meaning of symptoms in, 140; and finding personal direction, 53, 57; and healing, 23, 24; and humanness, 23; impairment in, 23–24; and inclusion, 126–127; mystery in, 30; outside of, reality and, 111–112; reciprocity in, 26–27; and relating to wholeness, 26; and relaxation, 31; resolving problems of mutuality through, 92–93; restoration of wholeness through, 65–67; role of, 23–24; therapist's silence within, 92; therapy in, 91–92; therapy outside of, 91–92; of touchstones, 111, 120–122

Directness, in the dialogical, 25

Disapproval, and confirmation, 97–100

Dissociative disorder, therapy for, 43–44

Distancing: case examples illustrating, 34–39; and common order, 102; as element of dialogical psychotherapy, 10–11; and relating, 10–11, 39–40; role of, in interaction, 32–33; ways of responding to, 37–39

Dreams: dialogue with, 72–73; elusiveness of, 70–71; as incomplete dialogues, 68–69, 71–72; meaning of, 71–72; possible origins of, 71; psychotherapy with, case examples of, 73–77

DSM-III-R diagnostic categories, 30, 46, 47, 143

Dysfunctionality, definition of, 8. *See also* Mental illness

E

Early childhood development, dialogical perspective on, 39–40

162

Index

Empathy, versus inclusion, 78–79
Empowerment, using unconscious
potential for, 62
Encounter: and personal direction,
52–53; and touchstones, 112. *See
also* Dialogue
Enmeshment, danger of, 87
Exhibitionism, treatment of, 142–
145
Existential guilt: case examples of,
105–109; definition of, 102–103;
discomfort of, 104; element of,
12–13, 102; finding source of,
109–110; and neurotic guilt, 12–
13, 105, 107–109; purpose in,
137–138; resolution of, 103–104;
and therapist's task, 105, 109–
110
Experimental psychology, 2
Exploitation, in therapeutic relationship, 87–89, 91–92

F

Farber, L. H., 7, 63
Fear: of acting, 45; existential, 20–
21; of people, 47–48
Feelings: being cut off from, 36–37;
in therapeutic relationship, 86–
87
Forgetfulness: healing of, 65–67;
sources of, 63–64
Fragmentation, of wholeness:
danger of, 148–149; definability
of, 17; discomfort of, 63–64; and
feelings, 36–37; and forgetfulness, 63–64; healing for, 42–43,
65–67; and loss of personal direction, 53; as mental illness, 42;
and reflection, 62; in relating to
self, 26–27; and the unconscious,
58, 63–67. *See also* Wholeness,
personal
Friedman, M. S., 7, 8, 10, 16, 24, 25,
39, 42, 50, 58, 59, 63, 68, 70, 71,
86, 110, 111, 122, 125, 153
Frustration, and dream work, 74–76

G

Gender dysphoria. *See*
Transsexuality

Growth: avoidance of, 119–120;
from interhuman contacts, 80
Guilt. *See* Existential guilt; Neurotic guilt

H

Healers: as dialogical, 155; varieties
of, 24. *See also* Therapists
Healing: barriers to scientific analysis of, 150–152; versus curing,
42; inobservability of, 152;
through meeting, 11, 41–49,
152–155; versus technique, 151;
uniqueness of, 152
Heard, W. G., 58
Human beings: common order
among, 102–103; extended dependency of, 87–88; fragmentation of, 148; and interaction, 32,
153
Hycner, R. H., 10, 39, 58, 63, 68, 72

I

"I," and existential guilt, 103–104
Identification, versus inclusion, 78–
79
I-It relationships: and analysis, 72;
and description versus experience, 26; and fragmentation,
17–18; historical development
of, 39; nature of, 33–34; in scientific world, 3; as source of mental illness, 34–37, 44, 149–151;
using theoretical orientation, 30.
See also Analysis, limitations of
Illumination, to resolve existential
guilt, 103
"Imagining the real," 12, 78. *See
also* Inclusion
Inadequacy, feelings of: healing of,
44; psychological defense
against, 64–65
Inauthenticity, source of, 114–115.
See also Seeming
Inclusion: clients' resistance to,
130–131, 132–133; clinical implications of, 126–127; and confir-

stones, 114, 121–122. *See also*
Client-Therapist relationship
Thickening the distance, 33, 38
Touchstones: adoption of others',
149–151; case examples using,
114–121, 149–151; dialogue of,
120–121; element of, 13, 110; as
essence of individual, 113–114;
evolutionary nature of, 112–113;
and reality of the between, 111–
112
Transference, 21, 87
Transsexuality, 55–56, 82–84
Treatment goals, in dialogical versus traditional psychotherapy,
137–138
Treatment process, in dialogical
versus traditional psychotherapy, 142–156
Trüb, H., 59, 63
Trust, in therapeutic dialogue: inability to, 130–132; need for, 91;
silence as betrayal of, 92

U

Uncertainty: in dialogue, 113–114,
140; in seeking personal direction, 95, 116–120; self-protection
from, 60
Unconscious, the: as aborted psychic activities, 65–67; access to,
62–63; case examples using, 60–
62, 63–65; as element of dialogical psychotherapy, 11; functions
of, 58–59; as guardian of wholeness, 62–65; mystery of, 68; as
personal wholeness, 59–62; ways

of viewing, 59–69. *See also*
Dreams
Unfinished business, and dreams,
76. *See also* Dreams
Uniqueness, personal, 1; and diagnosis, 135–137; and dialogical
psychotherapy, 9–10, 28, 125–
126; and personal direction, 50–
52; and touchstones, 113–114;
and the unconscious, 59
Unresponsiveness, of clients, 60–61.
See also Clients

V

Vulnerability: of clients, 87–88; of
dependents, 87

W

Wholeness, personal, 8–9; acceptance of, 80–81; actualized in the
between, 59–60; and existential
guilt, 104; and feelings, 36–37;
and genuine dialogue, 26, 28, 29,
65–67; growth required for, 60;
and inclusion, 79–80; instances
of, 17; and meaning of dreams,
71–72; mirroring of, 80, 92; need
for, 16–18; ontology of, 62–63;
and personal direction, 11, 53,
57; philosophy of, 7–8; power of,
case example of, 146–148; realizing potential of, 44, 59, 68; regaining of, case example of,
142–145; and relating to self, 26–
27; and the unconscious, 56, 59–
65, 68. *See also* Fragmentation,
of wholeness